D0463469

MY SON JOHNNY

My Son Johnny

JOHN EDMUND HAGGAI

Kobrey Press
Atlanta, Georgia

PREFACE

THIS BOOK is a tribute to two people ... to Christine, my wife, and to Johnny, our son. Christine will first hear about its being in print when she reads or hears prepublication announcements. Though the project started out as a joint effort, Chris felt impelled to abandon it. Emotionally it was too demanding. I was disappointed at first, but after several months I rejoiced. Because I saw that the book could be a tribute to her (and indeed it ought to be), I decided to complete it myself. According to his doctors, Chris's care for Johnny added years to his life. Her devotion to Christ through all the heartache, a devotion she would never agree to mention if she were co-authoring the book, could be used by God to inspire and challenge other parents who also suffer.

My purpose in writing has been fourfold. First, I want to indicate how God can use anyone, no matter how handicapped, if Christ is Lord of that life. Second, I want to challenge those who are discouraged, who are faltering, to move on to their maximum potential. Third, I want to show how God can use a beautiful, talented person to touch the lives of millions, even though her freedom has been restricted through a tragedy that has victimized her child and kept her confined to the home—and thus outwardly appeared to limit her ministry. Fourth, I want to demonstrate that some of the most profound work for God is the least known. Few people are called to withstand for a quarter of a century the pressures to which Christine was subjected. Yet the Haggai Institute would not be in existence today without her unique commitment. She served quietly behind the scenes. In a day when to many people bigness means effectiveness and loudness means achievement, her example refreshingly censors that fallacy.

Only someone who has lived through a family situation like ours can grasp how traumatic the writing of a book like this can be. Ken Anderson, a close friend, spent days in America and in Ireland, interviewing, assessing, recording the experiences of Johnny's family and intimate friends. He prepared the basic draft, and without him the book would never have been written. His quiet but vital involvement has been one of the most eloquent expressions of Christlike love and compassion I have observed over the course of my life and ministry. He was able to understand and feel as though he were part of our family.

Johnny could neither talk nor write during his

twenty-four years. At last, through this volume, he has the opportunity to communicate—oh, how he could communicate!—with the people across the world whom he loved and prayed for.

In addition to those mentioned in the book, I am sure Johnny would want me to express his special love and appreciation for Doctors Samuel Perry, Robert Gibbs, and Perry White (and wife Katherine), as well as evangelist Eddie Lieberman, his wife Grace, and daughter Flora Jean.

I want to pay special tribute to my mother, who was one of the first to realize the grasp of Johnny's understanding—that his mental competence was unrelated to his verbal incompetence.

I am so grateful for the sensitive insights and compassionate encouragement of Dr. Victor Oliver, editor-in-chief of Tyndale House when this project was begun, but now vice president in charge of North American affairs for the Haggai Institute. Helpful, too, has been Virginia Muir, managing editor of Tyndale House, who has made positive suggestions.

Special thanks are due to Mrs. Lanny (Margaret) Mauzy, who typed the basic draft, and to Miss Norma Byrd and Mrs. Velma Brown for their superb secretarial assistance.

The preparation of this volume has been the most exhausting and painful assignment I have undertaken. I am glad it is over. I pray that the book will help to heal the hurts of those who read it. Above all, I pray it will give the Lord Jesus Christ the preeminence he had in Johnny's life.

John Edmund Haggai
Atlanta, Georgia
August, 1977

ONE

A S I WRITE these words, my son Johnny, our only child, lies dying. It must surely be rare, in any lifetime, for a person to endure more than once such an excruciating night. Under such circumstances we become our real selves, the cut of cloth perhaps unknown even to our nearest kin and peers. In my case, at least as some see me, I should be in much better control of my emotions. Cool and calculating, they call me. A man who never weeps, publicly or privately. Well, I'm not weeping now, not outwardly. Inside, however, deep deep inside, my heart aches with the stinging salt of utter anguish.

"John," an author friend of mine told me a few months ago, "you've got to write Johnny's story. You must begin it before he dies."

But I procrastinated, not wanting to confront reality. Now I realize I must put it off no longer. I owe it to Johnny. And to his mother, my wife Chris.

I'm on a Pan American 747, flying homeward from the South Pacific where God has opened many doors on behalf of ministry to the Third World.

Before I can finish this book, Johnny—who is about to observe his twenty-fourth birthday—will have slipped away. I need him. I can't afford to lose him, but I know that the time has come to give him up.

I shouldn't complain.

I don't, really.

He has outlived by nearly twenty years the most optimistic prognosis of doctors who attended him in early childhood.

When I boarded this flight for San Francisco, the passenger agent came to me. I'd never met him. He put his arm around me and said, "Dr. Haggai, I just want you to know we're with you, and we all hope your son's condition will improve." Unknown to me, friends in the land "down under" had alerted the flight crew.

Shortly after we reached cruising altitude, the chief stewardess in my section slipped quietly over to me. She's European, from someplace like Sweden or Germany. "We're very concerned about your son," she said quietly. "If there is anything we can do, anything at all, to make your trip more comfortable, please let us know."

You hear about the impersonal professionalism of people who serve the public. I've seen it often myself. But this night our sovereign God seems to have handpicked a crew to help me through some difficult hours. Perhaps they're responding similarly to others on board with special needs. I don't know. I'm just grateful, to God and to them, for what they're doing for me.

Usually I read as I fly, or make notes relevant to the expanding Third Word ministry, or catch up on some necessary details. Not tonight. I've been sitting for a long time, looking out into the darkness. There is no moon, only starlight. I can make out the pattern of clouds below.

My work involves many overseas flights every year, so I make lots of trips like this. On two or three occasions Chris and I have taken Johnny along. How he would love to be with me now. Daylight, pitch dark, it never mattered to Johnny—just so he was flying.

Jim Irwin, one of the men who walked on the moon and who unhesitatingly declares his faith in Christ, gave Johnny an autograph. That thoughtful gesture turned Johnny on to the space age. Whenever there was a televised launch—and especially a moon shot—Johnny wanted to park inches from the set, his wide eyes riveted to every detail. It made him ill sometimes, he got so tense waiting for news on crucial points of a flight, especially liftoff and splash-down.

What a guy. I wish I could introduce him to you. He has a mind like a computer. He's witty. He reaches out to people. He reaches, even more effectively, out and up to God.

No one, not even his mother, spends so many hours daily praying for world outreach. Few people, not even those closest to me and my ministry, so succinctly understand my vision, my compulsions. Nor can I point to a man anywhere to whom I look so often for an example to follow.

In compassion.

Dedication.

Patience. Especially patience. For, you see, though he's twenty-four years old, my son has never entered into a normal conversation. He can't talk. He has never played a round of golf. He can't walk. He has never taken anybody out to lunch. He can't feed himself. He has never tied a Windsor knot. He can't dress himself.

But, though deprived of faculties most people take for granted, Johnny is a powerful communicator. He reads people with penetrating accuracy, and he shares his reactions with me—many times guiding me to right associations, helping to shield me from opportunists. Together we've worked out a system of sounds and gestures through which Johnny voices his concerns, making known his likes and dislikes.

He has a two-word vocabulary: "yeah" meaning "yes," and "umn" meaning "no." He constantly tries to voice other words. I have no doubt at all that an eloquent vocabulary resides in his mind. His intonations, however inarticulate, always include the proper number of syllables. Beyond those, he speaks with his eyes, with varied shades of countenance on a face deep-riven from so many years of frustration and pain.

Pain.

I can't really lay bare Johnny's story even though I have experienced it and feel every facet of it so keenly. Johnny's story is really his mother's story.

The long hours they have spent together almost constantly for nearly a quarter of a century. The measureless sacrifices she has made, all the more meaningful to me and to Johnny because she doesn't consider them sacrifices.

Every man should be proud of his wife. I'm proud, exceedingly proud, but equally grateful. God chose to bless my life with the presence of a truly beautiful woman. In the days of the world-famous Phil Spitalney All-Girl Orchestra, Chris competed in a national talent search and was selected as top soloist in the southern regional Hour of Charm contest. Back in the early days of Tennessee Ernie Ford's career, when he was on the staff of a radio station in their hometown (Bristol, Virginia—she lived on the Virginia side, he on the Tennessee side), she also teamed with him on a number of occasions.

Yet, through these years with Johnny she has sublimated her talents, her personal wishes, on behalf of her son. He requires constant care.

Johnny knows that, and it frustrates him terribly. Can you imagine yourself as you now are—same mind, interests, inclinations, aspirations—but the total *you* imprisoned in a nonfunctioning body?

That's our Johnny.

In his entire lifetime we have never been able to leave him beyond the hearing of someone, usually his mother. He has extreme difficulty digesting his food. He suffers frequent nausea and would strangle without help.

Compounding his physical limitations are his mental frustrations. For example, he turns a quick eye toward any pretty girl who happens to pass his way.

Although I know him so well, I cannot fathom what it must be like to have the normal perceptiveness, the same drives as any youngblood in his early twenties, yet live enslaved in a body like Victor Hugo's Quasimodo. At least Quasimodo was only a creature of fiction. Johnny is real.

He loves public places. The airport. A shopping mall. Hotel lobbies. Roll his wheelchair into a secluded corner where he can catch full view of the passing crowd and he'll watch for as long as you leave him there.

Whatever is normal to the mind and eye and potential lifestyle of any decent and contemporary American male is similarly normal to Johnny. Except for his body.

These thoughts crisscross my mind as I sit here on board. I've never known time to pass more slowly.

I've cut my South Pacific schedule short because of word from home. Chris was with me overseas. Then we heard from Mother Barker. Johnny was desperately ill. Chris decided to return home immediately. I insisted on going with her, but she wouldn't hear of it, saying that I needed to stay on and finish my work. A few hours later I received an urgent call from one of my colleagues, saying that Johnny's condition had worsened. That's why I'm heading east. . . .

Pan Am offers a postmidnight dinner but I can't think of food. Even on normal flights I rarely eat, a procedure I've found helpful in beating jet lag.

I'm bone weary. Yet I have no feeling of depression or sadness. Oh, I can be sad, but I hardly know what depression is. The Lord delivered me from that years ago, bringing out of the deliverance my book *How to Win Over Worry*.

With all my soul I believe in the sovereignty of a living God—that everything rests in his hands. That doesn't relieve me of responsibility, to be sure, but as I talk with him, as I seek to do his will, I can be confident that everything will work out for the very best.

Absolutely everything.

I do get a little impatient at times (some of my close associates might edit that to read "very impatient"), but not depressed.

Tonight, however, I'm obsessed with an entirely new emotion. We've known times before when Johnny faced death, but there has never been a time quite like now. Now Johnny not only lies at death's door, but the door stands ajar.

I hope and pray he hangs on until I can see him again, that perhaps medication and the life support systems available today may give him even three or four more weeks. But I must reckon with the fact that he could die before this 747 puts down at San Francisco.

My wife and I were able to slip away a few days before I left on this trip. We talked a lot about Johnny. "Our ministry would never have become a fact had it not been for Johnny," I said one night.

"I know," Chris agreed.

"And for all you've done to help him," I added, "to lift the pressure off my shoulders."

For many years Johnny suffered convulsions. We would rush him to the hospital and watch as the doctor burrowed a needle into his center forehead to inject sodium amytal. He subsequently developed seizures, distracting in themselves but compounded for me because they most often occurred just after I left on an assignment—or from the excitement of having me return home. The doctor prescribed mysoline, which Chris administered as sparingly as possible. Johnny has become highly intolerant to medication.

This in itself, I think, conditioned both of us to accept pressures and disappointments greater than those imposed on the average person. We were young then, and we grew with the constant imminence of such demands. At times it was like walking on egg shells, or razor blades, but it all added up to unparalleled preparation for the work God had for us. Now there is the Haggai Institute, ministering to credentialed leaders of the Third World.

My own life has been enriched, but I've been particularly impressed with what God has done for Chris. And what God has done for me through her.

Earlier this year, for example, after Johnny had gone through several bad days, she slipped down to the study I have in our basement. "There's something I must tell you," she said. Chris is an extremely resolute person, yet I can't remember a time when I saw more determination in her eyes than I did then. "I know how concerned you are about Johnny," she went on. "The doctor has warned us that it's just a matter of time. This year, perhaps. But you must carry on your work. I don't want you to hold back on your commitments."

What a selfless attitude. That's why I've been able to schedule four overseas trips each year, including this one.

Haggai Institute, which holds training sessions several times annually in Singapore and other Third World centers, now touches the lives of many Third World Christian leaders every year. Through them, a growing roster of resourceful Institute alumni, leadership training programs have been developed all across Asia and Africa and into other strategic areas. It is consistently more productive to train Third World people in their own areas rather than uprooting them and exposing them to the vast cultural differences in the western world.

That ministry, dear to my heart and consuming much of my energy, time, and concern, is all in a kind of limbo tonight. I have appointments to keep in the Middle East, India, Indonesia. Tonight, however, even though I'm far away, belongs to Johnny.

It's past time for him to die. That is his destiny. But I keep praying he'll live until I can get home, that his mind will be clear so he can recognize me. One more time I want to exchange those deeply personal moods of rapport that mean so much to both of us.

Do let Johnny live, O God! Let him live a few days longer.

At last we land in Honolulu and I make my way to a telephone. "You can't believe how weak he is," Chris tells me. "We almost lost him just half an hour ago."

"Do you have special nurses on duty?" I ask.

"Yes, I finally called for some help last night."

Her words strike me. Chris is by nature so frugal, so conservative, I know that she wouldn't have asked for relief unless she genuinely feared for Johnny's life.

"Something wonderful has happened," she continues. "Remember Dr. Buchanan? He heard you speak at Rotary here in Atlanta. Dr. Gibbs [Johnny's doctor] mentioned Johnny's condition to Dr. Buchanan, so he came on his day off to help us. Johnny has an intestinal blockage. Dr. Buchanan specializes in that kind of problem. They've inserted tubes all over Johnny's body. He's taking glucose and oxygen."

"I'm getting home as fast as I can, Sweetheart!"

"I know. But God has his own timing."

Back on board, I'm spectator to an astrophenomenon. The horizon all the way around us is a glorious pink. I've seen many beautifully lighted cloud formations from aircraft windows, but nothing quite like this.

Over and over in my mind go the words of the song, "When we shall meet to part no more."

It would be appropriate for our wonderful Creator, whom Johnny loves so devotedly, to herald his homecoming with such a spectacle.

As I had boarded the plane out of Honolulu the agent had taken me aside. The airline had notified him of my situation. "We'd like to accommodate you in first class," he said, "but we aren't allowed to upgrade passengers anymore. There's a fine of several thousand dollars if we do. But we have blocked out three seats for you in a nonsmoking area so you can get some rest between here and San Francisco." There is a continuing touch of concern on this trip that seems considerably beyond the call of duty.

There also seem to be familiar faces along the way. In the Clipper Club at Honolulu a businessman, one of the Lord's own, came up and said he remembered me from a crusade I once held in Peoria, Illinois. We had a time of cherished fellowship together.

I stretch out for awhile, sleep a bit, and now we are about two hours out of San Francisco. Occasionally, when I fly, I ask for a Bible. It sometimes opens interesting conversations, opportunities to witness. So when the stewardess comes by, I ask if they have a Bible on board. (Of course, I carry one in my briefcase.) She brings me a copy.

Within moments the Flight Service Director comes. "I was curious why anyone would ask for a Bible," he says. "It doesn't happen very often." I gesture for him to sit. After a moment's conversation I learn that he too knows and loves the Lord. He has recently been in Manila and is puzzled by the interest in "psychic surgery" there. We spend some time talking about the need for perceptiveness about what is the work of Light and what comes from the powers of darkness.

I tell him about Johnny.

"Oh, I'm so very sorry," he says. "I'll be praying for him, and for you."

I thank him.

"You know and I know," he continues, "that we don't need to have any special place for prayer. We can be working. We can be anyplace."

I have a time of rich fellowship with this man, my brother.

I'm back home now, in Atlanta. It was grand seeing Johnny again, but it also tore my heart. The haggard look in his eyes, the volumes of pain deep-etched all across his face.

"He's going to pull through," Chris told me when I entered the hospital room, "for now."

For now.

A few more days, another week. A month. But the certain mold is cast. The ever-tightening circle of pain. The rapid spending of his breath, his courageous heart. It can't possibly be for long, but at least we still have him with us.

Thank God!

I wanted to tell Johnny about my recent experiences, tell him about the scores of people who sent their love, their prayers. (Johnny was recently named honorary chairman of our Youth Adult Fellowship "down under.") But he's much too ill for extended conversation.

"Sure do love you, Buddy," I whispered to him.

I read a thousand words into the way he looked up at me.

My heart is full, as it's never been before. Johnny's life with us has largely been private, but now I am telling you his story, in tribute to Johnny and out of respect for his courageous mother. And because I believe Johnny has much to tell you.

TWO

IT'S ALL OVER now for Johnny. He's home at last with the Lord he loved and wanted to serve. Eternally free from having his young body an arena of almost constant suffering.

I could begin recounting his life by telling of his death, but it's the preceding life that determines whether death becomes an event of importance or an incidental happening. You will understand what I say as you read on, but I dare to tell you that Johnny lived a life of unique significance. Otherwise this book would have no purpose, and I could not have been persuaded to write it.

Let me begin the story at the beginning.

Back in 1943 the Lord had permitted Chris Barker to become a successful vocalist, but she wanted to use her talents for God's glory rather than personal acclaim. Thinking of attending Chicago's Moody Bible

Institute, she thumbed through the current student annual. One of the photographs immediately fascinated her. My photograph. She showed it to her mother—a woman who eventually came to live with us in 1955. She is not only my mother-in-law but also my cherished friend. When her mother took that first look at my photograph, her reaction to the foreign look of my countenance was quite unfavorable.

That incident in Christine Barker's life was almost forgotten when she arrived on the Moody Bible Institute campus. But when she attended a Monday morning convocation in the old Torrey-Gray auditorium, she had opportunity to observe the personification of the photograph that had caught her eye. Her heart sank. First, she scarcely recognized me from the picture. Then, though she had never been very racially conscious, Chris saw what her mother had seen initially but she had missed. I was indeed quite "foreign."

My background is Syrian, half-Syrian to be exact. My father came from Syria, my mother from a British-American background. I have long had to admit, however, that the map on my face is not London, it's Damascus.

In her first observation Chris summed me up as being from some "off-brand" Christian denomination and, a stalwart Baptist herself, she knew she could never entertain another serious thought about me. She put me completely out of her mind.

Chris says that once she was on the school elevator with me, just the two of us, but that I paid her no attention. On another occasion I don't recall, she says we brushed shoulders on the street. It wasn't that I was impervious to a beautiful young lady. It was pre-occupation, perhaps so-called absent-mindedness.

What I do remember is this: the first time I saw her, I flipped.

The sequence was this. My cousin, Margaret Haggai Johnson, also a student at Moody, said to me one day, "John, I just met a darling girl from Bristol, Virginia. A real southern belle." I informed her that women were not a part of my life until I finished my education. I asserted my intention to eliminate all dating until my studies were completed.

One Saturday morning, waiting for the taxi to take me to the train station for a weekend preaching assignment, I saw Marge and this beautiful young woman coming down the steps of the Moody Post Office. Marge introduced us, and then they went into the snack shop. Casually, but very much on purpose, I walked in front of that snack shop as often as the time lapse until the taxi's arrival permitted.

We fell in love, and I proposed to Chris on our third date. My dad was somewhat upset, asking why I would propose on the third date. "It seemed as though the second date was a little too soon," I told him.

The Barker family took the news with mixed reactions. Mrs. Barker (Mother Barker, as we call her) had grave reservations. Chris's sister Louise wrote, "I can't imagine having a sister by the name of Christine Haggai." Chris let me read the letter as we waited for the invocation at chapel one morning. I fumed. Her father, however, accepted me right away. He was an attractive man, the kind of person you turn to look at a second time. I regret not having had a chance to know him better. He died in 1946, slightly more than a year after Chris and I were married.

The pro and con of family reaction neither decided nor deterred Chris's decision. She wanted God's will for her life. And, looking back, I see that God had a special role for her to fill in the working out of his will for me.

On August 3, 1945, we were married.

After Moody I went to Furman University, where I held a student pastorate in Jackson Mills, South Carolina. Then I received a call from the Second Baptist Church in Lancaster, South Carolina. The church had just gone through the paroxysm of a split, leaving it with many problems. Yet God blessed it, and it began to grow. Attendance at prayer meetings, which had been averaging twenty-five to thirty, mushroomed to an average of nearly 300 per week. Sunday after Sunday, and often during the week, people were coming to Christ.

Once we brought in Jack Wyrtzen for a special evangelistic emphasis. In the somewhat cloistered confines of the Southern Baptist constituency in those years, few people had heard of Jack. But through vigorous promotion we had the place jammed, with some hundred people outside unable to get in. There were over seventy professed conversions that night.

Though scarcely more than an upstart in the ministry, I forayed beyond congregational boundary lines. Even then I believed that the church should address itself to the total community and not simply to the faithful comfortably ensconced within the sheepfold.

In those days the liquor industry crusaded from

community to community in a relentless effort to eliminate the "drys." Our church joined forces with other congregations in Lancaster to keep out the liquor stores. If the people of a given area could summon enough protest, they could keep their community dry.

One fellow came to Lancaster, intending to open a store near our church. "Ever heard of John Haggai?" someone asked.

To which the invader retorted, "Who the hell is John Haggai?"

He purchased property, brought in a truckload of stock, announced a grand opening. But we launched an all-out drive for signatures and had him closed down within thirty-six hours.

Chris and I talked about starting a family and became somewhat perplexed when three years passed without conception. Then in 1949, when I returned from some church business out of town, Chris greeted me with radiant happiness. "I'm pregnant," she said simply.

Her announcement awakened in me an emotion completely without precedent. The thought of our own child brought me up short with a new realization of the obligation and its meaning in marriage. Though I continued to program my mind with new plans and ideas for my work, I retained a glowing satisfaction of anticipated fatherhood.

And then suddenly our joy was shattered. Miscarriage. I questioned my wife cautiously as we returned from the hospital, trying to measure the depth of her disappointment. She was resting in God's will, she told me simply. To which I added, in what I did not then realize was a kind of prophecy, "But God's will isn't always easy to understand, is it?"

As time passed, I sensed my wife's concern. Would she become pregnant again? If so, could she sustain a normal pregnancy?

As our church grew, and particularly as word got around that our growing membership consisted largely of new converts, I began receiving invitations to conduct evangelistic meetings for other congregations. During a series of such meetings in Camden, South Carolina, we obtained some medical information.

Chris had recently told me she might be pregnant again, and when I asked her to go with me, she hesitated.

"Please come," I urged.

Reluctantly she agreed.

The meetings went well. Chris made many new friends, including one woman with whom she felt at liberty to share her anticipation. And apprehension.

"There's an excellent doctor in Columbia," her new friend told her. "He's highly recommended by the O.B.-Gyn department at Johns Hopkins University. He's had unusual success helping women through potentially difficult pregnancies."

Chris shared the news with me.

"Let's go see him as soon as I close this crusade," I said.

By the time we returned home, however, Chris realized she had been mistaken about the pregnancy.

"Let's go see the specialist in Columbia anyway," I insisted.

"Maybe it's no use," she said, discouragement full

upon her face. "Maybe we'll never be able to have a child."

"According to your friend in Camden, this doctor can help us."

After a full examination the gynecologist told my wife he saw no reason for her not being able to bear a child, a hymn of joy to our ears.

"When she does become pregnant," I asked, "would it be safe for my wife to come to Columbia for consultations?"

"What is it," the doctor asked, "an hour's drive from your home? That shouldn't pose any problems."

The specialist was a delightful man, an urbane and engaging conversationalist. We subsequently learned that women came from all over North America, sometimes from all over the world, to consult him. In fact, about the time of our initial consultation, we read of a woman from one of Europe's prominent royal families who came to Columbia specifically to seek his help.

From her first appointment, he treated Chris like a daughter.

"I get the feeling God has a special reason for our meeting this man," she told me.

"He's got a very special patient," I said.

"I had a chance to witness to him today," she said after one appointment.

"What was his response?"

"He listened. I'm sure I detected deep spiritual hunger in his eyes."

What we didn't know then was that this doctor had had an only son, a Navy pilot shot down and killed during the Korean War. The stricken father sustained an outward appearance of acceptance, but inside he suffered anguish with which he could not cope. More and more he had allegedly begun turning to alcohol for relief.

Anticipating a confirmed pregnancy, Chris made frequent visits to Columbia and felt increasingly constrained to trust God for opportunities to relate her faith to her specialist.

Months passed.

Yet no pregnancy.

My wife prayed and prayed.

Wondered.

We prayed earnestly, importunately.

It took many anxious, unrewarded months. But the following year, 1950, my wife told me she strongly suspected she was with child.

"Let's go to Columbia right away!" I said.

We did.

And she was.

"You be careful, young lady," the specialist cautioned. "Do exactly as I tell you. To reward your efforts, in about eight more months we'll have a new member in your family."

Chris gave me exuberant reports of her visits to the doctor. Again and again opportunity for witness presented itself. Each time he became more attentive. She longed to see him open the door of his heart to the One who stood waiting there.

Our life abounded with happiness.

"You know, Sweetheart," I told her one day. "I've never seen you more beautiful."

Several months later she told me, "I think we're going to have a boy. With no previous experience to compare, I can't say for sure, but this little one kicks like a football star. Only I think he's more interested in being a preacher. I'm sure I can feel him trying to pound on a pulpit."

We laughed together in our great mutual joy.

At a ministerial meeting one day, one of the men came to me and said, "I hear your wife's expecting."

"You hear correctly," I told him.

"We just had a son, you know," he continued. "People ask if I want him to go into the ministry. I sure hope not. I'd like to see him become a doctor."

I shook my head and said, "If the Lord gives us a son, I can think of him only in the highest possible calling, a preacher of the gospel."

"That's two of us, Honey," my wife said when I related the incident to her later in the day.

"I pray he'll come to Christ at an early age," I mused, "and that the Lord will let me be around when he makes his commitment."

"You take charge of his commitment," Chris said pleasantly, "but I'd like to be the one who leads him to the Lord."

"Maybe we can do it together," I suggested, again unaware of the prophetic implications of what I'd said.

"I'll need to ask you to have the baby in one of the hospitals here in Columbia," the specialist said as we discussed the delivery.

Everything proceeded beautifully. The doctor gave Chris detailed instructions for every moment of her pregnancy. We were concerned at first lest there be another miscarriage, but as the time lengthened we became more and more confident and joyfully anticipant. I called frequently from the church office or wherever I might happen to be. Whenever possible, I worked at home.

Now Chris looks back and realizes that the Lord began preparing her in advance for the uniqueness of our child's birth. For example, like any expectant mother, she purchased many things the baby would need.

"What is it this time?" I asked, as I saw a large box she placed with the other things.

"A playpen," she told me.

"Open it," I asked. "Let's have a look."

But she didn't, diverting our conversation, and I didn't make an issue of it.

The next day, after I had gone to my office at the church, Chris went to the box. Of course she should open it, she reasoned, and see if everything was in order. Yet, she thought, suppose something happened and she didn't need it. We were watching our pennies carefully and would want to be able to return things without difficulty.

Late that Sunday afternoon, as I got ready to leave for the evening service, Chris felt sure it was time to go to the hospital. I moved quickly into action, having made plans in advance for both the church program and our own activity.

I notified the hospital and placed a call to the doctor. The doctor wasn't home. "I've got to talk to him," I insisted. "It's my wife. She's ready for delivery. Tell me where I can get in touch with him."

Whoever was on the other end of the line made an obvious effort to minimize my concern.

"Look," I continued, "I know it's Sunday. But tell

the doctor my wife's in labor. I've alerted the hospital. We're on our way this moment, and it won't take us an hour. Be sure he's there when we arrive."

I snatched up the suitcase Chris had packed in readiness and escorted her to the car. We quickly dispatched the miles between Lancaster and Columbia.

"Is our doctor here?" I asked, as we pulled up to the emergency entrance and an orderly stepped out.

"I don't know," he said, "but they can tell you inside."

Inside, I learned the doctor not only had not come but had made no contact with the hospital.

"That's probably because he's on his way," Chris said.

I went to a telephone, but could get neither the doctor nor any assurance that he was coming.

"There should be no reason at all for alarm," a nurse assured us. "Doctors routinely have patients come to the hospital this way, at the first sign of labor. Then they arrive in ample time for the delivery."

"You keep the doctor informed?" I asked.

"Of course," she said.

"You'll have to get him to the phone first," I told her. "I can't."

"He'll probably be in touch with us momentarily, giving us his point of contact," the nurse said. "It's Sunday, you know."

They took Chris into a room, and I felt encouragement watching the careful pains they took to make her comfortable.

"Just push the call button if you need anything at all," the nurse said, and left.

The doctor didn't check in with the hospital. Nor did any of my efforts to reach him by phone succeed.

Just as I was about at the end of my wits, one of the nurses came in and said, "The doctor just called. We gave him a complete report and he assured us everything was routine. He'll keep in touch with us."

"Keep in touch with us?" I fumed. "What kind of specialist is that? He should be here!"

"Has he indicated anything unusual to you about the pregnancy?" the nurse asked.

We admitted he hadn't.

"Then he'll be here when he's needed."

Time dragged on.

My wife became increasingly distressed.

But for some reason, the doctor who had taken such a reassuring interest in our case became unexplainably aloof.

It was one of the longest nights I can remember.

THREE

CRUCIAL HOURS they surely were. For Chris, who bore the brunt of the physical ordeal, but also for both of us. Our personal lives, my career, our marriage—all would be altered by the events of this grueling night.

The nurses got Chris up and walked her through the corridor. I watched, concerned for every step she took.

"Has the doctor called?" I asked the nurse. I glanced at my watch. Three o'clock in the morning.

The nurse shook her head and began walking away.

I reached out and caught her sleeve. "Is this really routine," I wanted to know, "the way he's handling this case?"

She didn't answer. But I thought I saw in her eyes something of the concern evident in my own.

For as long as I've known my wife, she has been almost the complete opposite of a hypochondriac. That night, though, there was no hiding the pain. I felt incredibly helpless. I knew Chris needed me as a source of comfort, not to intensify her plight. I took her hand and prayed silently, urgently, for the Lord's intervention on our behalf.

The doctor did not come.

When at last morning dawned and time came for Monday office hours, I renewed my efforts at the telephone.

"The doctor isn't in yet," his nurse told me when I finally reached his office.

"But my wife has been in labor all night," I said. "Can't you somehow find him?"

My circle of close friends includes more medical doctors than people of any other profession. I respect them. The years they spend in training, its financial cost, the way they deprive themselves of activities normal for others their age—all that makes me tolerant of many things others chafe about. We thank God for the physicians and surgeons who stand with us in our Third World ministry. But I can never understand those few men I have encountered, men literally capable of holding your life in their hands, who can somehow remain nonchalant, if not actually indifferent, in times of great need. It's as if they're more interested in leasing an empty store in their shopping mall to tenants than making an appointment to meet physical need.

I went to the new head nurse on duty. "Look," I said, trying to remain calm. "I've kept trying to call our doctor. He's the reason we came to your hospital. Can you locate him for me?"

"We'll try," the nurse said. "You go back to your wife. I'll let you know as soon as we know."

Chris was in great pain. It tore my heart watching her. I remember again taking her hand, trying to pray. She jerked her hand away, clasped both hands to her face.

I turned to go back to the telephone. The head nurse met me at the door.

"Did you locate the doctor?" I asked.

She nodded and gestured for me to slip out into the hall.

"Is he coming?" I asked as we stood there alone.

"I don't quite understand it," she said. "I only got his receptionist. She told me the doctor was in his office, but was too busy to come to the hospital."

I exploded. I grabbed the phone and once again dialed the doctor's office. "Will you please put the doctor on the phone right now?" I asked his receptionist. "I've got to talk to him!"

"He's with a patient," the woman told me. "The best I can do is have him call you back. Please give me the number of the phone where you are now speaking."

I gave it to her. But he didn't call back.

It was incredible, absolutely and utterly incredible. Like the most cruel dream of a lifetime, a dream from which one is ecstatically relieved to awaken. Only I knew I was already awake.

"You can't tell me this is routine care of a patient!" I complained to the head nurse.

"Labor can be quite prolonged when it's the first delivery."

"This prolonged?"

She came to the room and checked my wife's chart.

She had been properly professional, skilled at handling the impatience of a first-time father. Now, however, I saw her register alarm.

"This doctor delivers babies here?" I asked.

"Of course," she said nervously, "several times a week."

"With this same kind of conduct?"

She stood mute, flustered. I hesitated a moment and bolted once again for a telephone. This time I got through to the specialist. "I want you here right away!" I insisted.

"I'll keep in close touch with the nurses," he said nonchalantly, ignoring my anger. "They have an excellent staff. They can take care of your wife."

Frankly, he was so cool about it all, so convincing, that I felt a tinge of shame. I went to the room. Chris was awake, aware of the pain but under considerable sedation.

"When do you think the baby will be born?" I asked the nurse who looked into the room.

"We can't be sure," she replied.

"Minutes?"

No answer.

"Hours?"

No answer.

"Is it likely to be soon? Yes or no?"

Still no answer.

I did a foolish thing. To keep myself from going crazy I went to the parking lot, got into my car, and headed back toward Lancaster. I'd spend some time at the church office and try to get my mind onto other things.

Five miles down the highway I realized the self-centeredness of my action. I turned back to the hospital.

Once more I got the specialist to the phone. "The reason we came to you in the first place," I told him, "was because we wanted you to be here for the delivery. I don't want assistants, nurses, hospital staff, I just want you—over here as fast as you can get here. I won't stand for another minute of delay."

"I'll be on my way shortly," he said.

"But if you're delayed, where do I call for you?"

"I'm coming now."

He didn't come immediately but he did come. He was curt, hasty, almost a different man from the competent gentleman we had learned to respect and trust. I should have detected the influence of alcohol. In my shock and disdain I didn't.

"There's very little dilation," he said, "I'll have an intern keep in touch with me. We could probably send her home."

"Send her home?" I exclaimed. "But she's been in labor so long!"

"Relax," he said, talking down to me in the old cliché, "we've never yet lost a father."

They got Chris out of bed and walked her up and down the corridor.

An intern occasionally looked into the room. I tried to hold my patience, but finally I again consulted the head nurse.

"We're doing everything we can for your wife," she said kindly.

I looked at my watch. "It's been over twenty-four hours," I said. "Don't you think about caesarean in times like this?" She smiled. "Don't you?" I prodded.

"It really does happen quite frequently that a woman experiences early labor pains with her first delivery," she said.

"This intense and prolonged?"

"Well . . ."

I went back to the telephone and again had difficulty locating the specialist. At his home they didn't know where he was. It was after hours but I tried his office, with no response from anyone. I called his home again. "Surely someone knows where he is," I pleaded, my anger giving way to fear for my wife and child.

"Is it an emergency?" the person at the phone asked.

"Yes, it is! Now please tell me where to reach the doctor."

At last I located him.

At a cocktail party.

He came to the hospital. But from the moment he walked into the room, it was now plain to see he had been drinking. Nevertheless, I felt relieved. He *was* there.

It was 9:00 P.M.

"Let's take her into the delivery room," the specialist told the nurse. That same nurse subsequently told me that, in his condition, he should never have been permitted on the premises.

It was a breech birth with complications. Had the doctor been on hand and alert earlier, had he been sober, he would surely have delivered the baby by a caesarean.

I waited impatiently outside the delivery room, pacing back and forth like a caged panther. Being a person of reasonable resourcefulness, I tend to put a lot of emphasis on problem solving. But here was a problem I could do nothing about at all.

The time dragged on. And on.

At last the doctor emerged. One look told me he was uneasy, that things hadn't gone well.

It was 10:00 P.M. the night of November 27, 1950.

"How's my wife?" I asked. "The baby?"

"Since you're a man of the cloth," he said, his head bobbing slightly, "I'll quote you something from Isaiah. 'He shall shave with a borrowed razor.'" He gave me a sickly grin, walked out into the night, and I never saw him again. The Old Testament quotation didn't make any sense to me then, and it doesn't now, not in that context. But it's true that when Johnny did come to manhood, his circumstances were such he could never shave himself.

I waited several more minutes and grew so impatient that I bolted toward the delivery room door.

"You can't go in there!" a nurse called out from somewhere.

"Watch me!" I called back.

Another doctor had come into the room, a country G.P. from Goldsboro, South Carolina. How I wish I could remember his name. Apparently a nurse, knowing he had come in to see one of his patients, summoned him to the scene. He quickly saw that both the baby and the mother needed urgent attention.

Chris opened her eyes weakly, momentarily aware of my presence, and closed them again.

"You have a son," one of the nurses whispered.

But I knew I had a son in trouble, as I watched the

doctor cross the little fellow's arms over his waist, then lift them high above his head. The baby became fire engine red, then pale, then blue.

"Do it again, Doctor!" I called out. "Do it again!"

"If I do it any more frequently," the doctor said, "it will kill him."

Little Johnny—though we had not yet selected his name—breathed only once every two and a half minutes for the first three hours.

"Why did our doctor go home," I asked, "with our baby in this condition?"

"He probably didn't expect the child to survive," someone said in a muted voice probably not meant for me to hear.

You can't understand unless you've experienced something like that—looking on, knowing how desperate the situation was, unable to do a thing.

Except pray.

And that I did, though not so earnestly as I might have. I was so disgusted and disillusioned, if not downright infuriated, that my mind was a quagmire.

Others in that room, I later learned, also prayed. God had placed on duty a missionary nurse home on furlough. And the delivery room staff also included a missions volunteer from Columbia Bible College.

We needed prayer, much prayer.

"I'm willing to put my entire career on the line," the nurse supervisor told me. "This is the most inexcusably bad delivery I've ever seen. If you want to sue for malpractice, I'll be your prime witness."

Malpractice.

"Won't our son be all right?" I asked anxiously.

The nurse lowered her eyes.

"Please tell me," I prodded. "I can take it."

"Your doctor hardly knew what he was doing. To be completely frank, he was drunk. You might as well have called for an automobile mechanic."

I subsequently learned that, because of the delay and because of inept procedure during delivery, our baby suffered cerebral hemorrhages causing extensive brain damage. His jaw was badly injured. Both collar bones were broken. His right leg was pulled apart at the growing center.

"He won't be normal?"

"If he lives," the nurse replied, in a tone of voice clearly indicating her doubts about the child's survival, "he'll be spastic."

I stumbled out of the room, half-angry, mostly numb. I saw in a blur as they brought Chris back to her room.

"I think she'll be okay," the country doctor told me, "but I've got to be honest with you. She suffered so badly it's possible we could lose her."

I remember pacing up and down the corridor, calling out to God.

It was an agonizing night. Even for a Christian, for one who thought he had so implicitly put everything into his Lord's hands. Even for one who heralded from the pulpit the abundant resources of grace and faith.

I called my dad, a clergyman. I should have consulted him before but had been too confused.

"We're in real problems," I told him, and explained.

His voice came back, calm and assuring, "You know, when you were a little boy and I was a pastor back in Middleville, Michigan, I made you a little kiddie car. I remember one day you rode it back and forth in front of my study door until you nearly drove me to distraction. You kept calling out 'Mah, Mah' to your mother. Well, *mah* is the Hebrew word for 'whatsoever.' That directed my attention that day to John 14, the thirteenth and fourteenth verses, and I came to a solution of the problem I was wrestling with. So, since you gave me that solution twenty-three years ago, I give it back to you now. '*Whatsoever* you shall ask in my name, that will I do, that the Father may be glorified in the Son.' And remember, I'll be spending the night in prayer."

Moments later a telephone call came for me. It was one of our deacons back at the church in Lancaster. "There are 200 people here in the sanctuary," he said, "and we'll be praying through the night for you and Chris and your son." How they got the news, I never knew.

Johnny's birth was the beginning of a long, strangely enriching, and maturing adventure.

FOUR

S THE COUNTRY DOCTOR had predicted, the ordeal left my wife debilitated. She didn't see and scarcely heard the baby in the delivery room. His plaintive cry, the abnormal way his chin receded, the leg that had to be put into a cast as soon as a doctor could get to it. It would have been too much for her to take in her weakened condition.

"Have they said anything to you about the baby?" I asked when I came into her room the next morning.

"They haven't brought him to me once," she complained.

"You've been very ill," I said.

"Is that the reason they haven't brought him?"

"He's having some difficulty breathing," I told her, "but they're taking care of it. He seems to be responding."

I had been advised not to worry my wife. But people rarely become adept at evasion, do they? As time wore on, as doctors and nurses kept putting Chris off when she asked about the baby, she read the evidence in their manner. She began grasping for any straw of hope, however slim or furtive, but found little encouragement.

Nurses are almost always a fine species of the human family. In our case they gave consistent extra effort to look after my wife, to make her as comfortable as possible. It seemed to her at times that they wanted to shed the outer veneer of professionalism and relate woman-to-woman. Whenever she tried to obtain specific information about the baby, however, they avoided the issue.

That is, all of them except Sudy. Sudy Waters. Ten years my wife's senior, a woman of wisdom and compassion, Sudy took a special interest in Chris and a special interest in our son. We later learned that, had it not been for the tireless hours Sudy spent with our boy, he would never have left the hospital alive.

When Chris asked other nurses about the baby they would quickly busy themselves fluffing her pillow or offering to rub her back. Or they would look for such trivia as a water glass needing to be filled. But when she asked Sudy, Sudy would stand by her bed and smile, her eyes full of concern and compassion as though her spirit reached out to Chris.

"Please tell me the truth about my son!" Chris implored one day. "I'm not a weak person. I'll be far better off if you tell me the truth than to have everyone avoid the subject when I ask."

Sudy took a deep breath. "He has difficulty breathing," she said.

"My husband told me that."

"It's—it's a very serious difficulty."

"How serious?"

"At times he becomes very blue, very dark, and we give him artificial respiration."

"And?" Chris primed, realizing she had not been told all.

"Your doctor should inform you," Sudy said, taking Chris's hand and stroking it gently.

"You know the situation with the doctor," Chris reminded her.

Sudy nodded. "I can tell you one thing," she said. "Your baby has a very beautiful body. All the nurses in O.B. who have seen him talk about it. Just beautiful." The nurse turned away.

"Please tell me!"

Slowly turning back, the nurse said, "At times he is quite spastic."

Spastic. The word was like a dagger struck deep into a young mother's heart. Chris closed her eyes and cried out in silence to the Lord. So many times she had given witness to others of the validity of His promises. Now, He was asking her to put those promises to the test.

She did put them to the test. Her nerves calmed, her courage strengthened in measures far beyond herself.

During those days in the hospital, she read the entire book of Psalms. Again and again as she read, she transposed her situation into the words of David as he cried out to God. She particularly remembers the birthday Psalm, the ninetieth, specifically the words: "We spend our years as a tale that is told. The days of our years are threescore years and ten; and if by reason of strength they be fourscore years, yet is their strength labor and sorrow; for it is soon cut off, and we fly away. . . . So teach us to number our days, that we may apply our hearts unto wisdom."

Somewhere beyond the walls of her room and kept apart from the normal babies, she knew that her child lay struggling for breath, his beautiful but broken body racked at times by spastic seizures.

She tried to visualize him, to let her imagination reach out and comfort him. What was he really like? What might his future be? She could only wonder, anxiously, through every waking hour. Her sleep was restless, troubled.

"So teach us to number our days. . . ."

"He's such a brave little fellow," Sudy would tell Chris during those treasured moments when she would slip into the room to report on his condition. "He's fighting hard."

"Will he live?" Chris asked.

"I can't say."

"But is there any chance?"

"Oh, yes, Mrs. Haggai! That's why we don't give up." How beautiful it was, the resolute honesty in Sudy's eyes, the compassion and hope in her voice, the determination.

"What is he like? I mean his face. What does he look like?"

"A real little preacher," Sudy said, giving vent to a brief moment of casual mirth. "He's the handsomest kid we've had in the last six months. That's why we keep him isolated. If we put him in with the other babies the boys would be jealous and the girls would all be crazy about him."

Chris cherished the words. She learned from that nurse, as much as she has ever learned from anyone, how important it is to reach out in love and encouragement to someone whose life has gone into a place of darkness. Sudy's words and Sudy's smile were like the flame of a candle flickering badly but burning brightly.

Those days remain a blur in my mind. I had to get back to the church, to my responsibilities. I prepared sermons and Bible studies, answered the phone, took care of correspondence—like an automaton.

As I look back now, however, I cannot remember ever yielding to despair. I don't lay claim to any special dimensions of spirituality, but what I can wholeheartedly affirm is that the promises of God are true. "My grace is sufficient for thee," our Lord declares, and it is true, experientially, for any child of His who finds himself or herself adrift in storm-tossed circumstances.

Under God, I wanted to be as effective a pulpiteer as possible. Dr. J. C. Massey, then well in his eighties and one of America's outstanding pulpit masters, challenged me to proclaim the all-sufficiency of our Lord so that people would be comforted. I remember his saying, "John, give the people some heaven on Sunday morning. They've had hell all week long." God had given me the joy of bringing comfort to people who were hurting, people in strangely unique circumstances.

So, of course, I had no idea how he was to prepare me through the life of Johnny. A new dimension came into my own experience and ministry, and I experienced, as we sing in the song, "the wonderful grace of Jesus." Undergirding. Empowering.

During the months of my wife's pregnancy, we had talked about a name for the baby. If a son, his name would be John Edmund Haggai, Jr.

Well, God gave us a son, but a son almost more dead than alive.

Monday passed.

Tuesday.

Wednesday.

"I guess we really should select a name," I said one evening when I drove over to see Chris. "I mean, we should tell them the baby's name is...." My voice trailed off. Suppose our son lived but became little more than a vegetable? In that case, why name him John Edmund, Jr., when we could save the name for a son who was normal?

Names are very meaningful to me. I've always cherished the simple anecdote about my own name. My parents had discussed the matter at length, particularly since names were more significant in our family than in the average American home.

My father was teaching in a Bible study series, and his theme was "The Grace of God." He and Mother were so convinced that the child she was carrying would be a girl that they determined to name her "Grace." When the unborn child was very much a boy, they named him "John," which means the same thing. When Mother was with child a second time, Dad was teaching a series on "The Gift of God," and again they were absolutely certain that this child would be a girl. They would name her Dorothy. Once again, the child turned out to be a boy. So they named him "Theodore," which means the same thing, the "gift of God."

Now, I was faced with the task of naming a son under considerably less pleasant circumstances.

"Should we first wait to see if the baby lives?" Chris asked.

"But we agreed," I replied, "that if we had a son, we would name him after me."

"Only then we didn't realize what the situation would be."

Glancing at my watch, I realized I needed to get back for an appointment. I left without our having arrived at a decision.

But that night, Thursday, the choir met for practice at the church. They wanted a report on the baby, so, after my appointment, I went into the sanctuary.

"Have you named the baby yet?" one of the women asked.

"We have," I said, surprised at my own words. Then without any hesitation I added, "He's John Edmund Haggai, Jr."

The choir broke into applause.

I told Chris first thing when I got back to the hospital the next afternoon.

"I'm so pleased," she said, smiling. Then she sobered, adding, "But I'm also troubled."

"About what?"

At such a time, I think any sensitive Christian is driven to a certain amount of introspection, as Chris was then, trying to determine whether there is anything in his life or her life that isn't pleasing to the Lord. So I reminded her of the New Testament account of the man who had been born blind, and how the people asked Jesus whether or not the parents' sins had caused the man's blindness. "Remember," I told her. "Jesus said it was so the glory of God could be more fully revealed." Then I added, "But I've been doing the same thing."

We're sinners, all of us—saved only by the grace of God. That I clearly recognized then (as I clearly recognize it now). Yet to the best of my knowledge there was nothing we were holding back from the Lord. In those beautiful moments of sharing, of complete openness, we dedicated our Johnny to him. "We place him by faith on your altar," I prayed. "If it's your will that he die, take him. But if it can be possible in your sovereign will, we ask you to heal him. If he lives, whatever the circumstances, we trust you to show us your plan for his life."

Chris wept quietly for a few moments. I had known her before this experience as a person of quality and strength. That's one of the reasons I married her. But now I began to see new depth and resilience in her personality, her character.

"I wish I could see him," she said. "I seem to remember just one glimpse in the delivery room. I'm not quite sure."

"They can't bring him," I tried to explain, "because he needs constant care."

"I understand," she said.

I could understand why the nurses had refrained from letting Chris see the baby. But why hadn't they let me see him? I went to the floor supervisor. "I want to see our baby," I said.

"That's not possible," she replied. Then, like a condescending parent talking down to a child, she added, "You need to spend all the time you can with your wife. Frankly, Mr. Haggai, if she doesn't have a real good cry, she's going to crack up."

"My wife is undergirded by the strength and peace only Christ can give," I said.

The woman shrugged her shoulders. She turned away to some other things on her desk, ignoring me.

"When can I see the baby?" I asked.

She looked up. "I told you—"

"Look," I interrupted, "I'm a clergyman. If you can't let me see him as his father, then you must let me see him as his pastor."

She was caught completely off guard by that.

"I want to offer a prayer for the child," I said.

I had won my case. A student nurse was summoned, told to give me a sterilized coat and mask, and to take me to Johnny.

Sudy Waters was there, just the two of us with the child.

"He's such a dear baby," she said quietly.

But I didn't see a dear baby. I saw a helpless infant struggling for every breath, the marks of injury plain across his little body. I'm not sure whether in that moment I wished him dead or alive. Across my mind flashed the face of the specialist, the man who had robbed my son of his rightful beginning in life. Anger grew like a fire in my thoughts.

Then I remembered the counsels of my father, a giant in the faith among all the great men I have known. Quietly, but with strength and persuasion, he had challenged me to find God's sure will in this experience, to settle for nothing less.

I bowed my head. I don't remember the words I prayed. I know only that I dared to believe that my Lord was sovereign in the valley as well as on the mountaintop and that I could place my son with complete confidence in his care.

"It was beautiful, Mrs. Haggai," Sudy Waters later told my wife. "I felt as though I stood on holy ground!"

"You did stand on holy ground, Sudy!" Chris exclaimed. "You surely did."

FIVE

LTHOUGH Chris remained in the hospital only a week, they kept Johnny a month. In all that time she didn't see him, let alone hold him. Every waking moment became a torment of concern and longing and frustrated loneliness. He was flesh of her flesh, son of her heart, yet torn from her.

My own thoughts became increasingly tormented as I began to retrospect and thereby widen my perspective of what had happened in the delivery room. To this day I have no doubt that the specialist, the man in whom we had put our trust, was guilty of malpractice.

Yet can you understand the conflict I sensed at the prospect of a malpractice suit? Though I was advised to proceed with one, I couldn't bring myself to do it. This man was a craftsman, a brilliant, world-famed specialist. This was simply an exception. Suing him for malpractice wouldn't in any way help Johnny. On the other hand, I was sure that when he realized the tragedy he had created, it would sober him literally and figuratively.

When one thinks of the Cross, and how many have flouted the God who created them and who has provided redemption for them, the God who loves them deeply and redemptively and eternally—well, under these conditions a malpractice suit was unthinkable.

I must confess that on occasion I was nettled when one doctor in particular, in an obvious effort to protect those of his fraternity, said, "Your son wasn't injured at birth. He simply suffered a maldevelopmental midline defect." Of course, that doctor was totally wrong; the preponderance of evidence neutralizes his nonmedical and nonscientific and nonfactual assertion.

I also had another concern: my wife was often treated as much like a child as was our baby. It seems to be common medical practice with many to keep facts away from patients, even if they are of reasonable intelligence and normal emotional qualifications. Hospital personnel, except for Sudy Waters, simply refused to give us information. (I do know some doctors who make a point of carefully explaining to their patients the significant details of both diagnosis and therapy. May their tribe increase!)

At times we got the impression our son might live a few months or, at the outset, a very few years, but would exist in a kind of comatose state. He would be blind, totally deaf, unable to recognize us. During his first months, those anguished days and hours and weeks of not knowing, we both learned many new lessons in trust.

The experiences of Job became especially meaningful. We could understand his cry: "He knows the way that I take. When he has tried me, I shall come forth as gold."

My second sermon in "practice preaching" at school was on the subject of suffering. I surely had no idea then how prophetic in my own life the material of that early message would become. In the pastorate and in special meetings during my evangelistic ministry, God seemed to use messages on suffering in a remarkable way. My thesis was that suffering is the only constant in this world. Paul told the Philippians: "For unto you it is given in the behalf of Christ, not only to believe on him, but also to suffer for his sake." And Paul reminded his spiritual son Timothy that "all that will live godly in Christ Jesus shall suffer persecution. . . . If we suffer, we shall also reign with him."

To be sure, life for a Christian consists of much joy. "Weeping may endure for a night," the Psalmist sang, "but joy comes in the morning."

Suffering reveals itself in a variety of profiles.

Even the hypochondriac suffers. Imagined illness can evoke mental responses that become intensely uncomfortable and painful. And of course many people suffer real physical pain. But there is still another dimension.

I'm privileged to work with many outstanding Christian businessmen, such as the men who make up the board of the Haggai Institute. Every one of them can relate experiences in which he paid a price to maintain a consistent Christian lifestyle.

For example, take young Jerry Nims, founder and president of Infinioptic, Inc., which has developed a new approach to multidimensional photography. Jerry's innovation applies not only to still photography but to motion pictures and even X-rays. He has been offered millions of dollars in backing, including a very large sum from the publisher of America's best-known pornographic magazine, if he would relinquish just part of the rights on this new invention.

But Jerry plans to make sure his product will not be used in any manner that does not honor the Lord. Thus, although he could have had access to ample funds for development, he chose the slow, laborious route of growth. For a young businessman, eager to surge ahead with the greatest possible momentum, that's suffering. And God will always bring glory to himself, and give blessing to his child, from that kind of suffering.

I hesitate to describe our experiences with Johnny as "suffering." I prefer simply to tell the story, to make clear to you why those twenty-four years became a time of joy to us. However, at least in the sense of normal human evaluation, we did undergo personal hardships. The Lord permitted us that experience and we accepted it as such.

But never mind the suffering. It was a time of great joy for Chris the morning the phone rang and she was told we could come to the hospital and get the baby.

"It's going to be rather complicated for you," the nurse said. "We'll need to take some time to show you care procedures."

I'm sure Chris heard the words only numbly, so great came the surge of anticipation to her heart. When we had advanced to within mere footsteps of seeing our son, she was trembling.

"Just over here," the nurse said softly, guiding us to a room separate from the glassed-in nursery section. There stood Sudy Waters, with Johnny propped up in a bassinet. She held his head in her hand as she force-fed him with a Brecht feeder, a device that forced milk down his throat much the same way you would feed a little bird with a syringe. The feeder was like a baby bottle with a plunger at one end and a nipple at the other.

"I thought I should introduce you right away to the procedure of feeding Johnny," Sudy said. "We use this device to compensate for the paralysis of Johnny's throat muscles. He isn't able to form his lips or manipulate his tongue to operate the nipple. This feeder squirts the milk into his mouth and down his throat. It helps him swallow."

Chris stepped up for a closer look, asking, "Will I ever be able to master it?"

"Of course you will," Sudy encouraged her. "It does take some skill not to give him too much milk, or you'll strangle him. And not too little, or he'll take in air. But you'll catch on to it."

There was something so reassuring in Sudy's voice and manner that it put Chris greatly at ease. She drew closer for an even better look at Johnny. "He's handsome, John," she said grinning. "He looks just like you." I winced.

As I stood looking at our son (and I know it was the same with my wife) I had nothing like a sense of despair, even though I knew we had a severely injured child. The chances were remote of his ever living a normal existence, but what characterized both Chris and me was acceptance of Johnny. We wanted him. He was God's gift to us.

Hospital medical authorities, however, gave us a grim diagnosis of Johnny's condition as well as an entirely bleak prognosis for his future.

"Put him in an institution," they advised. "What's the point of a young couple in your mid-twenties tying yourselves down to the care of such an unfortunate little creature? He won't know the difference— whether *you* look after him or some institutional staff worker trained to cope with children in his condition."

The suggestion never took so much as a moment's root in Chris's mind. Johnny was our baby, flesh of our flesh. We wanted him if he could only look up at us once a day; if, in all the weeks or months—or, God allowing, perhaps years we would spend together— he might just once gladden our hearts with a smile.

Hospital staff members gave Chris extensive directions, but always with a note of negativism. She drank in every word, eager to do her best for our boy. Still, they expected her to be back in a few days, to run into trouble and perhaps lose the boy before we could rush him all the way from Lancaster to Columbia. And if Chris did manage to master all the chores, they presumed we would grow weary and before long commit him to an institution.

Even Sudy Waters was less than optimistic, warning that "the Brecht method becomes more complicated when the child is ready for solid food."

Those people simply didn't know my wife. She is a

person of tremendous emotional sensitivity and spiritual commitment, a person who has almost a passion against imposing on anyone or inconveniencing anyone. People would sometimes offer her a gift and she wouldn't want to take it. I would urge her to take it, reminding her that there is a grace to receiving as well as to giving.

When it comes to giving herself for others, however, that's a different story. For our son she was willing, if not actually eager, to pour out whatever measure of herself might be required on his behalf.

(We subsequently sought clinical assistance in many places. At the University of Pennsylvania, for example, we were told: "There is no case on medical record where a child as badly injured at birth as yours has lived more than five years." News like that cut my wife to the heart, but at the same time it heightened her determination to do her utmost for Johnny.)

"The doctor questions whether he sees or hears," Sudy told my wife. Even from Sudy's gentle lips, the words hurt.

"Is it normal for a baby his age?" Chris asked hopefully.

Sudy didn't answer. Instead she hurried about to collect his things and get him ready to leave.

I didn't hear what Sudy said, nor did Chris tell me as we drove back to Lancaster. It was pointless to tell anyone. She didn't believe it was true.

Chris's mother had arranged to be on hand when the baby arrived. She met us at the door. "Anything I can do?" she asked.

"Not unless you want the honor of putting the first diaper on your grandson," Chris told her.

"That would be a special honor," Mother Barker exclaimed, sweeping the child gently out of his mother's arms. "You see, I've got everything ready over here on the table."

Chris found an undergirding reassurance in her mother's attitude, an outflowing of love to the new baby.

"Such a sweet little face," Johnny's grandmother would say.

But however much we loved the child, we couldn't find many evidences of alertness. He lay limp wherever Chris placed him, eyes closed most of the time. If he cried, it was only a whimper—more like a strange, inhuman noise than a living sound. Chris spent hours holding him, watching him.

The first time we took him to the hospital for a checkup, the doctor said, "I must be very frank. Your child will always be abnormal."

"How abnormal?" Chris asked.

"You must think of yourself, your husband, and family," he said, bypassing her question. "You mustn't let yourself be saddled with the responsibility."

We arranged for testing by a psychologist. "Your boy is a vegetable, and he will always be a vegetable," he told my wife.

Chris remained undaunted. She is a strong-willed woman, but she is also a Christian who places high priority on being sensitive to the purposes of God. The Lord had placed in her a subliminal awareness that our Johnny had been sent into the world with work to do.

Mother Barker did the most to sustain Chris's courage. She could remain with us only for short periods of time while her own aged father lived, but during those intervals she filled our home with joy and optimism. She chatted to Johnny, sang to him, and treated him as though he were a completely normal grandchild.

As months passed, Johnny developed an acute breathing problem. You could hear him all over the house. We wondered if it would get progressively worse until he suffocated.

"It might help to remove his adenoids," the doctor said, with very little encouragement in his voice.

The operation was performed, the results were excellent, and our optimism was sustained. In all honesty, however, when weeks and months passed without any noticeable improvement in Johnny's mental growth, we did look into the possibility of placing him in an institution.

"What do you think we should do?" I asked my wife one day.

"If we place him in an institution," she answered, "he'll die in a very short time."

It was Chris who showed the most confidence and courage. At that time, of course, neither of us suspected how important our son would become to our Third World ministry. But Chris knew, profoundly, that the Lord had made no mistake when he sent this child to us. Neither of us fully realized what she had committed herself to. "I want to keep the baby right here at home," she said.

"It will mean constant care," I said.

"I'm prepared to give him constant care."

"Day and night?"

"Day and night."

And so began the long tolling of the years.

We kept in close touch with doctors. Eventually I felt God's call to a church in Chattanooga, where we were able to place Johnny under the care of an excellent specialist. Chris told the doctor about every little evidence indicating that our son was sensitive and alert. The kind doctor only smiled and gently shook his head.

Then one day as Chris held Johnny after feeding him, he opened his eyes.

"Watch my finger," she whispered, moving her hand back and forth just above him.

Mother Barker was visiting at the time, and Chris called out to her, "Watch his eyes as I move my finger!"

"He feels, too," Mother Barker said. "I stuck him with a pin, changing him yesterday, and he opened his eyes wide."

Chris related the exciting news to me. "He sees and hears too," she said.

"You sure?"

"I was taking the wrapping off some dry cleaning." (Cleaning firms used paper instead of plastic in those days.) "He was asleep. He heard the paper rattling and awakened."

"Terrific!"

"Maybe he's going to make the doctors all wrong. Maybe he'll improve and improve."

She watched the baby more closely than ever those next days, and became increasingly assured of his growing alertness. "Do you notice how he registers interest whenever he hears your voice?" she asked me one evening.

So I began talking, walking back and forth in the room to test him.

"He's following you ever so little with his eyes," she exclaimed.

"You sure?" I asked. "About my voice too?"

"I first noticed it yesterday. He was restless. Then you came home. You didn't even come into the room, but he heard your voice and it quieted him." No one can erase from my memory the satisfaction of those words.

Though Chris took excellent care of Johnny and became sensitive to his smallest need, she determined from the outset not to spoil him. He did need constant care. She could never be beyond hearing him and, preferably, never even beyond view. But she wouldn't let concern and responsibility deteriorate into needless and harmful pampering.

She tried singing. Of course it was only natural for her to want to sing around the house. But initially Johnny would have nothing of it. Even if he heard her off in another room, he would fret. Actually, Chris had to give up professional singing almost entirely. It was more than ten years before she could resume training with her new and excellent voice coach, Gertrude MacFarland. That was very difficult for her to accept.

She had every reason, humanly speaking, to chafe at times, wondering why the Lord would confine her that way, taking away opportunities to serve him publicly. She couldn't even attend church regularly.

She found recourse in her Bible, sincerely seeking to lay bare her heart to the counsel and guidance she found in God's Word.

Meanwhile, the move to Chattanooga was not a happy experience for me. God gave us some wonderful friends with whom we're still in contact, but the Chattanooga pastorate turned out to be a time of much testing.

"Some of these people are hopelessly intransigent," I fumed.

Chris asked me if I thought we should have stayed in Lancaster. I had second thoughts about that question myself.

I tried to placate my frustrations with activity. I plunged into interchurch affairs and began a radio ministry. Often I left the house at five in the morning for a 5:45 broadcast. Sometimes church activities would keep me occupied at full speed until past midnight. It seemed that every day would bring a new epidemic of problems. That would put a strain on any marriage—and we could have faced a real crisis.

"Did you have to book radio time at such an unearthly hour?" Chris complained.

"Five forty-five in the morning is the only time the station has available," I told her. "Besides, I've observed that the majority of successful people are up early. They are goal oriented, achievement motivated, and decisive. Too often they're not challenged, at their level, to move out to their ultimate potential for God. Those are the people I want to relate to—doctors, farmers, top businessmen—challenging them to put God first."

It was also meaningful to me that the radio signal

reached much farther that hour of the morning. My father, for example, heard me all the way in Binghamton, New York, even though I was on only a 5,000-watt station.

The early hour was a real problem for Chris. Johnny, who invariably wakened early no matter how late it was before he got to sleep, seemed to hear the slightest movement about the house. He became particularly alert to any movement made by me. One step at the head of the stairs, near the door to Johnny's bedroom, squeaked loudly whenever you put your weight on it and never so loudly as at 5:00 A.M.! At the first sound of my footstep, Johnny awakened with his strange, plaintive cry.

Invariably Chris would have been up with him during the night. (In fact, during those first years with Johnny, she never had more than two hours of uninterrupted sleep, day or night.) I tried every way I could think of to negotiate that step on the stairs without disturbing our son. One morning Chris became vaguely aware of my being up and, dead tired though she was, waited to hear the creak on the stairs, knowing it would trigger Johnny's cry.

She heard nothing.

Curious, she raised herself on her elbow and looked out the door. There she saw her husband, flat on his stomach, inching his way down the stairs and negotiating the creaky step without a sound.

No matter what ploys we tried, Johnny continued awakening early, sometimes as early as 4 A.M. In the summertime, we could keep the house tolerable at night only by opening the windows. As Johnny grew older, he began to awaken in the happy mood of any baby. He learned to make sounds and make them loudly. Morning after morning Chris would have to go quiet him. Otherwise, through the open window, his loud voice would disturb the neighborhood.

We finally invested in a room air conditioner, considered very much a luxury by people those days but a distinct necessity in Johnny's case.

Chris became more and more weary. Some days she performed her chores like a robot.

"I *would* have to take the most difficult pastorate in the South," I lamented, "right when I need to be helping you."

"I'm managing," she said.

I was proud of her for her courage and often spoke about it to those I encountered during the day. "She's an incredible woman," I would say.

One night when I returned home from a meeting, I slipped quietly into the house and found her weeping. I was at a loss for words for a moment. Then I said, "I know it's rough on you."

But she wasn't weeping for herself. Johnny had had an especially bad day. She pointed to him and whispered, "To see him suffer so."

It took years before I fully understood the price my wife paid on our son's behalf. She had to call upon the Lord constantly just to get menial activities of the day accomplished. Looking back, I realize I could have been a lot more helpful.

"I know I'm not the easiest person to live with," I often told Chris.

I guess I'm what you would call a "workaholic," a high-octane driver, goal oriented, with an unusual ability for preoccupation when I get on some project. That isn't easy for a wife to contend with. There would be times when Chris would tell me something significant, and I would appear to be listening but not hear a word.

I have tried through the years to keep her fully informed, particularly as new ministries developed beyond the pastorate. I shared blessings, of course, but I also shared problems and difficulties. For more than twenty-five years she was the only person with whom I discussed the negatives in my work. I never have believed in advertising deficiencies. A thorough optimist, I prefer to keep people informed of the positives, the successes.

I always gave my wife a detailed schedule of my time so she could quickly get in touch with me. There is not a thirty-minute segment, during my overseas assignments, when she doesn't know where I am. Even if I'm overseas, should my schedule change, I always send her a telegram or call her by telephone. She knows airplane flight numbers, estimated time of departure and arrival, who will pick me up, how I will be transported, where I will stay.

When Congressman Mendel Rivers was alive (he was chairman of the Congressional Armed Forces Committee), he told me, "John, I keep a red telephone in my car, at my desk, by my bed. If in an emergency you ever need to get in touch with the States, you just go to the nearest military installation and get me on the red phone. I consider your work that strategic." I never used that facility but it was a comfort to know I could rely on it.

I also took out more insurance than a man of my means would ordinarily do, because I wanted Chris to be protected.

I was caught up in a momentum that sometimes saw every day giving rise to new potentials, new opportunities. And Chris, wonderfully and patiently, tried to accommodate her life to mine.

One day Dr. W. A. Criswell, beloved and respected Southern Baptist leader, came to Chattanooga. A man of large vision, he realized how heavily the difficulties in the Chattanooga church weighed upon me and impeded my vision and drive.

"You're a fine pastor, John," he commended, "but if I may pose as a prophet, I think you will outgrow the pastorate. You need to consider evangelism."

Evangelism? I felt buoyed by the confidence this world-renowned leader had placed in me. At the same time I felt no attraction whatever to a full-time itinerant ministry.

SIX

IWELCOMED invitations for evangelistic crusades. While conducting a limited number, I also kept chipping away at the problems posed by my pastorate. Then I received a call to pastor a church in Louisville. I accepted it.

There, success seemed to touch every plan and program. The church led the entire Southern Baptist Convention in reported conversions and baptisms, 421 in a year's time. We saw remarkable growth in the Sunday school. In less than two years, our yearly budget rose from 90,000 dollars to nearly a quarter of a million.

As a result I was asked to speak at a pastor's conference of the Southern Baptist Convention in Kansas City. They gave me the first slot, Monday evening. Ordinarily at such a conference people are still arriving and unsettled on the first night. That year there was an hour and a half delay in starting the program, so many of the late arrivals, who otherwise would have missed that meeting, were on hand to hear me speak.

My message on "The Place of the Pulpit in Evangelism" got a response beyond my fondest anticipation. A report of the sermon appeared in hundreds of newspapers from the New York *Times* to the San Francisco *Chronicle*, sometimes on page one.

Within a few weeks I received over 400 invitations for meetings. It would have taken me more than twenty years to fill all those engagements. And in the weeks following, more came in. My father said, "I've been praying for years, John, that God would lead you into evangelism. I didn't say anything to you because I didn't want you to be influenced by me, only by the Lord."

The first invitations were from individual churches. But from one city, for example, I received requests from twenty-nine different congregations. Obviously, the solution was city-wide meetings.

So it was decided: full-time evangelism.

I felt like a new man. Chris says even my voice seemed different, as though I had overnight gained the stature of many maturing years.

"I wish you could have been with me," I told her after one of the first crusades. "God gave me freedom and authority in preaching. There were more than 200 people who professed faith. It was a simple gospel message. No pressure. No emotionalism."

No pressure?

No emotion?

I saw the hurt in my wife's eyes. In my enthusiasm I could so easily overlook her pressure, her emotional problems.

"You sure we shouldn't find a place for Johnny?" I asked one day. "Then you could travel with me."

She shook her head.

"You can't go on like this," I said.

"You know what the doctor says. Now that he's lived this long, the most we can expect to have him for is five or six more years. I can manage that."

The work became increasingly difficult for Chris. Then her grandfather died, and Mother Barker visited more frequently. "I fall more in love with Johnny each time I'm with him," she said. "If you'd like me to, I'll come full-time to help take care of him."

I suppose any man would be apprehensive about having his mother-in-law live in his house, but mine is a very special person. I count her not only as a cherished relative but as one of my finest friends and one of the people I deeply respect and admire.

About that time Chris became acquainted with a group of parents whose children needed various kinds of therapy. It was before the days of Salk vaccine, and polio stalked the country. Within the group also were parents whose children suffered from such disabilities as cerebral palsy. They met once a month, sharing experiences and ideas.

Through that group Chris learned about a therapist at one of the local hospitals. Chris and Mother Barker took Johnny to her. She showed them various exercises and told them of another specialist in Baltimore who had had unusual success in treating crippled children. We went to him, and he prescribed a home therapy program. One therapist tried to equip Johnny with braces so he might eventually move about on crutches.

"Do you really think there's a chance?" Chris asked, choking back hope and at the same time reaching out to it.

"He's got a lot of spunk," the therapist said.

Both of us had thought the braces on other children looked unsightly, if not ugly. But the braces the doctor fitted on Johnny's legs were works of art—except for their futility. We lifted Johnny upright and tried to encourage him to take a step, but his eager little brain couldn't give the simplest signal to his limbs. Chris worked at it tirelessly, hour upon hour, crying out to God that her boy might know something of the joys other children experience.

Our one gratification was an almost daily reinforcement of Chris's conviction of Johnny's intelligence. More and more we saw his body as a kind of chrysalis. If only it could have been so, if the butterfly within, awaiting advent of spring, could have burst forth in fulfilled glory! In reality, though, Johnny's body was nothing like a chrysalis. It was a prison.

One thing was sure, though: he was no vegetable, no mental incompetent. He was alert. Loving. Eager to learn. Capable. Chris tried little things like holding him on her lap and pointing out various objects in the house. He could never respond with great speed because the damage to his motor nervous system caused a twenty-second time lapse between his sensory perception and response. And twenty seconds can seem like a very long time. A less patient mother might have given up, never leading her child to the breakthrough of revealed intelligence.

But the breakthrough came for Johnny.

"Where is the fireplace?" his mother asked one day.

Johnny's eyes turned directly toward it and Chris's heart leaped in symphony. Wanting to be sure, she named other items. Radio. Piano. Dining room table. Clock. Johnny could identify them all. Then she taught him the parts of his body.

"He'll talk one of these days," she said to me.

I hid my skepticism in silence but profoundly admired her optimism.

"If he does talk," the doctors cautioned, "it'll probably be with much difficulty. His speech isn't likely to be fully articulated."

We could accept that. With his mother's help, we could learn to understand him, to know the unique shadings he might give to any word in his vocabulary. Even if he spoke another language Chris would have learned it, so desperately did she anticipate communication with her son.

Yet even as he never walked, so also he could not talk—except for the two expressions, "umn" and "yeah," which became slowly distinguishable in his otherwise inarticulate vocalizing. He recognized us, clearly and consistently. A glow of love came to his eyes. Because of his respiratory problems he was extremely susceptible to colds. As he grew older, the sound of a sneeze struck literal terror to his heart.

Chris made overt efforts to mingle love with the attention he needed. Mother Barker was especially good at that. It could be exasperating to guide him laboriously through a meal only to have him lose it. Any person might be forgiven for showing impatience. Except for the look in Johnny's eyes. There was first of all the distress, but deeper than that, the frustration. It was an uncomfortable experience, and as the years progressed increasingly nerve-racking. Yet how deeply his mother understood. The thought of reproving him was completely alien to her mind.

Johnny's condition was such that he could have been a very untidy child, but Chris kept him spotlessly clean. She had a way of doing it so he didn't feel put upon. She had an amazing capacity for keeping him well groomed but accomplished that feat without making a big production of it.

The more time she spent with him, the more convinced she became of his intelligence. How thankful she was that the Lord did not permit her to listen to those doctors who questioned Johnny's mental ability. If she had, she would never have discovered it. She would never have known how to enrich his life.

"I know Johnny has at least normal intelligence," she would say. "It's possible that he has higher than normal intelligence."

One cannot help wondering what Johnny might have done with his intelligence. Could it be that he inherited his mother's gift of music? With his boundless spirit, might he have sung the praises of the Lord? Would he have followed in my footsteps? For many years I've sensed the need for a young man to work directly at my side, helping me with details as well as with the broader opportunities of our ministry. Might that young man have been Johnny? I think he also asked such questions.

For, though Johnny couldn't speak, he could articulate volumes through his expressive eyes. Reading those eyes, we learned many things.

His eyes underscored his sincerity when he called for help. It was never the call of a pampered child. No, he summoned help only when he had honest need. That was part of his integrity. So, although caring for our son did involve long hours of effort and continuing deprivation, it was also a time of personal enrichment for his mother.

Happiness requires reaching out to other people, guiding them, doing your share to widen their horizons. That was certainly to be the role of Johnny's mother.

Johnny was a prisoner, locked in the fetters of his impotent body. His mother's task—I've heard her insist it was a privilege—was to find ways by which he could even partially escape from that prison. The more his mother lived with him, the more she consulted her Bible and communed with her Lord, the more convinced she became that Johnny Haggai was a child of destiny for this world. It was a long, long ordeal. But I too am convinced that God gave Chris the privilege of teaching one of his own choice children. Who are we to question the *why* of our son's physical imprisonment as that prison became—as I shall explain—an arena of worldwide exploits, a sanctuary of purpose and praise?

SEVEN

THE SCRIPTURAL IDEAL for life demands growth—growth in "wisdom and stature, and in favor with God and man." Johnny was to increase only threefold. In wisdom. In favor with God. In favor with man. He was denied one of life's foremost assets, a sound body. As the months passed, we watched him experience phases of the normal stages of childhood. Internally normal, I should say. Externally, abnormal.

He saw us walk about the room.

Sit.

Stand.

Move our arms.

Pick up objects with our hands.

He wanted to emulate all of it. God knows how

deeply it hurt to see Johnny struggle to manipulate his body. Deep in his eyes we saw the longing to stand and walk and reach out to touch and hold. Full across his face appeared his anguish as, with the passing of time, he realized that the world of normal people was not to be his world. But he cherished that world.

As he grew older we took him outside, sometimes for rides in the car. More frequently Chris or Mother Barker would push him along the sidewalk in his stroller. He wanted to be where people were. He would sit for hours watching children play, squealing with delight at their antics, lurching his twisted little body at the sight of a baseball bat swinging, growing tense in the exciting moments of a basketball game.

Always we kept probing, searching out any possibility by which we might bring him closer to the norms of life.

For example, when he was a very small child we introduced him to therapy. If you have observed the care of severely handicapped children, you may know about patterning. It is a procedure in which the therapist guides the limbs of a child in the simulation of a crawl—somewhat the same as in swimming—until the child's mind adapts to the action and he is able to take over by himself. Multitudes of children who would otherwise have been immobile for life have learned at least to crawl through the patterning process.

For Johnny, patterning therapy demanded a much more extensive procedure. To achieve any results at all, the therapist told us, Johnny would need to have sessions five times daily. They could be conducted at home. It took five women at a time, however, a total of twenty-five in all, for one day's sessions. Mrs. W. J. (Sammie) Brooks, a lovely person and loyal friend, recruited people for us. Most women could come for just one session each week, so the total number in our volunteer force amounted to over one hundred women each week. But Chris still expedited much of the therapy herself.

Johnny tried hard to achieve. No athlete in Olympic competition ever tried more strenuously to win. How he struggled, with resolution in his eyes!

He did learn to crawl, just a little. But patterning was of benefit beyond its specific intent. When Johnny subsequently began to develop severe osteoporosis*, the doctor told us that his bones might have gone to powder without that exercise therapy.

Later we secured a costly patterning machine, which tended to manhandle Johnny rather uncomfortably. Yet he did his best to accommodate. Like us, he seemed to envision continued improvement in his physical condition. He was willing to extend any effort, however uncomfortable or painful and for whatever length of time, to achieve improvement.

"You're a real trouper, Buddy!" I would tell him, and he would glow in response.

Our highest hope with patterning was that we could develop substitute nerve pathways to bypass the damaged ones, so he could learn to walk. In 1965, however, after two years of fruitless striving, we gave up.

I think Johnny was relieved. And, like us, disappointed.

*A condition in which there is a decrease in bone mass and density, resulting in porosity and fragility of the bone.

But though he lacked in physical talent, he showed increasing aptitude for developing his mind. Chris introduced him to as many experiences as possible. She taught him the fragrance of flowers. He seemed to have a normal sense of touch and she let him feel as well as see various objects in the house. He discovered the different textures of cloth. He learned colors. He became keenly sensitive to different sounds, inside the house and outside.

We had some fine neighbors, parents of lovely children. One of the girls, a little younger than Johnny, came in almost daily to see him. Some mornings he fretted so much that Chris had to scold him. But let the doorbell ring, and his little friend arrive, and he became all smiles.

On his fourth birthday Chris gave him a party. She made it as gala an occasion as budget and ingenuity would allow. Neighborhood children came and played. Chris served cake and ice cream. From the time the children arrived until they left, the twinkle never faded from Johnny's eyes.

We made much of Christmas. Chris decorated the tree and other areas of the house, especially Johnny's room. At Easter she colored eggs and she made May baskets. We took Johnny to see Fourth of July fireworks. We tried to make sure he never missed a parade. We filled his life as full as we knew how to fill it.

When he was two years old, we bought him a cocker spaniel. Johnny wanted to be on the floor with the dog as much as possible, and Chris often found them curled up together, sound asleep.

In fact, Johnny developed quite an affinity for dogs.

Even strange dogs took to him, as though they recognized his plight and wanted to cheer him, to protect him.

We had a neighbor by the name of Ollie Merchant, who wouldn't permit dogs on his property—with one exception. A mongrel pup in the neighborhood loved Johnny. When Johnny was outside with Mr. Merchant, and only then, that dog would come running to the Merchants' back yard. There he curled up beside Johnny's chair. As soon as Johnny went home, the dog quietly slipped away without being told.

Another neighbor had a fine boxer who would appear whenever Chris rolled Johnny out onto our patio. That dog became very protective of him. When the dog died and the neighbors got another to replace him, an identical relationship developed.

Duke, another neighbor's pet, was the last dog in Johnny's life. Nothing seemed to taste quite so good to Duke as a morsel of food taken from Johnny's hand.

The Lord taught us wonderful lessons in the worth of just one human spirit in those years. Might it be a stroke of Satan's own genius that causes so many people—yes, even Christians—to disdain anything less than physical wholeness as subworthy in the human family?

Again and again Chris said, "I'm so thankful we didn't listen to the counsel of all the people who told us we shouldn't keep Johnny."

One doctor, for example, told her, "Lady, why don't you sublimate this martyr complex of yours and have the child put into an institution? You're going to spoil your own life, perhaps ruin your marriage, and jeopardize any future family you might have."

But only a few months later, as the therapy I have just described was in full operation, medical attitudes began to change.

"He's very cooperative," one therapist admitted. "We've established that he has surprisingly excellent comprehension. He clearly understands what we want him to do. The only problem is his acute lack of physical coordination."

Chris spent hours trying to help Johnny develop that coordination. During the early years she went through all the routines of building blocks, trying to help him put round circles into round holes, fit square pieces into square holes. You could see how clearly he understood what needed to be done but he simply couldn't get his fingers to coordinate.

Chris always remained positive with him. "We'll practice on this some other day," she would say when failure upon failure with some project utterly unnerved him. "This is a skill we can learn later."

As he grew older, Johnny developed even more severe gastrointestinal problems.

"Could it be because he becomes so frustrated?" Chris asked the doctor.

The doctor nodded. "It not only could be the reason, Mrs. Haggai; it *is* the reason."

So should we have institutionalized him? Pushed him off into a corner of some ward where he would lie, day after day, staring up at the ceiling? Might that not have been better than continually introducing him to a way of life he could never experience for himself? Heartless questions.

Knowing Johnny as we came so intimately to know him, we are sure that an institution would have shortened his life by ten years or more. With his keen mind and profound sensitivity, he would have experienced enormously more frustration than that imposed by his efforts to learn and to express himself. In an institution he would have been in a prison within a prison.

Still, with the passing of time the dimensions of his terrible imprisonment became more and more obvious. Medicine helped his debilitating seizures, although he always had extreme difficulty in taking it orally and keeping it in his stomach.

My schedule grew increasingly demanding. I tried to organize my work, however, so I could spend as much time as possible with my family. I should have done more. But having a child like Johnny is one of those experiences where you become wise in retrospect.

Several doctors have volunteered the firm belief that Chris was the one responsible for the extension of his life. Every day was an ordeal for Johnny but some days were worse than others. On especially bad days, Chris would often be on her feet from morning until night. Though she was not the kind to indulge in self-pity, times came when massive weariness made it impossible for her to restrain her tears.

One time, after several hours of activity, she took a few moments to sit and relax. But Johnny needed to be watched, so she placed him in her lap. Tears began to flow down her cheeks. Johnny saw the tears and responded with a nervous laugh.

Another day—so tired, so completely at nerves' end—she broke into outright sobbing. Johnny responded with an outburst of laughter. You've perhaps seen a child who falters between laughter and tears. That's the way it was that day with Johnny. Chris remembers bringing herself up short on that occasion, wiping away the tears. Then she began to sing the simple words of "Jesus Loves Me," a song Johnny always responded to with glowing enthusiasm.

"He does love us, Johnny," she whispered, holding his face against hers. "He loves us! Very much."

After Mother Barker came, Chris could get away on occasion. She never would have survived otherwise. But the maternal instinct in her ran deep. She felt a keen responsibility to her son. It was impossible for her, at least in those initial years, to break away for any extended time.

With Mother Barker's coming, and as Johnny grew older, Chris resumed voice lessons. She even began to make public appearances. I always considered it a highlight of one of my crusades to have her on the program.

Fortunately, Johnny had reversed his attitude toward his mother's music. Now he encouraged her to sing, sometimes trying to sing with her in his enthusiastic, if totally inarticulate monotone.

We are the stewards of our time and talents; both are gifts of God. Among her many commendable attitudes toward life, Chris has always believed that tomorrow's opportunities will be lost unless we prepare for them today. We've met parents of normal children who, in our opinion, handicap them by not stimulating them to rise to their fullest potential. If our children are to grow up as purposeful Christians, their minds need to be carefully programmed in childhood. You reap what you sow in the minds of your children. But sowing and nurturing take time. Unfortunately, too many parents look to television as the time-occupier for their offspring.

My wife believes that God gives us children as life's supreme investment. At different ages in a child's life, we have increasing opportunities for Bible teaching and spiritual example which can potentially touch future generations. By our influence over one child, she contends it is possible to have a larger share of the future than, for example, by teaching a Bible class, important as that may be.

Though she hardly knew what it was that motivated her to be so intent upon Johnny's care, she would one day realize what a great plan God had for our son. It was his mother's responsibility and opportunity to help prepare him for the fulfillment of that plan. God give us more mothers and fathers who rear their children with more than an attitude of "feed them, clothe them, get them out of the house."

Chris becomes a bit impatient with women who lament not being able to teach in Sunday school because of their children. Because of their children? What a pitiful attitude, to ignore one's greatest opportunity and responsibility. Measure up to your parental potential with just one child and you will project your influence far beyond your years. With two or more children, the equation multiplies.

But we must be careful. Our families become our first responsibility, my wife believes, but never should that responsibility become an excuse for not fulfilling our total responsibility within God's plan for our lives. In spite of the long and laborious hours required with Johnny, Chris found time for other important things. With her fine sense of decor and innate capacity for neatness, she maintained our home with loving care. Having had to give up her music for a time, she could easily have slipped into persistent sullenness because of the burdens imposed upon her. But God gave her grace, and people visiting the home would consistently remark about her radiance. They came to bless and left blessed themselves.

Chris was good about keeping me informed of Johnny's progress, his visits to doctors and therapists. But she tried not to let any problems get in the way of my ministry. For example, I was conducting evangelistic meetings at the Hunter Street Baptist Church in Birmingham, Alabama, when one of the women assisting Chris with Johnny's therapy unintentionally used too much force and snapped Johnny's femur. Because of his condition, a broken bone created considerable crisis. Chris knew, however, that I was about to go into the pulpit and waited until after the meeting to call me. I came right home.

Over and over again she absorbed most of the pressure in order that my ministry not be hindered. People across the country and the world have heard me say that next to my salvation, the greatest thing that ever happened to me was meeting and marrying Chris. Without her I could never have fulfilled the ministry God has made possible for me.

From Johnny's earliest childhood, Chris encouraged him to show interest in his father. I spent time with him whenever I could, but I was never with him for long blocks of time the way Chris and Mother Barker were.

"Now let's get you all cleaned up before your daddy comes home," Chris would say if Johnny had had trouble with food. "He likes young preachers who are clean and neat."

"Yeah," Johnny would say.

Johnny's affinity for me grew far beyond the bounds my wife had imagined. We grew so close, in fact, that she could have easily been tempted to resent our relationship. She would look after our son, hour in and hour out, but at the sound of my footsteps Johnny forgot everyone's presence in anticipation of his father's appearance.

It wasn't easy for Chris to see me taking advantage of my opportunities, enjoying my successes, my freedom. Who was to say that her singing might not have contributed as much, or more, to the cause of Christ than my preaching and pastoral activities? Had the situation been reversed, in no measure could I have been as tolerant and as gracious as she has been. Occasionally it was too much, and she would indulge in visible, sometimes audible expressions of disappointment.

But Chris found a personal fortress in the promises of the Bible. "My strength is made perfect in weakness," our Lord assures us. We don't need to be some kind of awesome saint to have divine provision operative in our lives. We need only to "grow in grace, through the knowledge of our Lord and Savior, Jesus Christ." Commitment, in its most accurate definition, exposes our weaknesses to his strength.

Well, since we both believed in the adequacy of God's provision, why not ask him to perform a miracle of healing? We most certainly did ask God to touch

Johnny's body—but only according to his sovereign will for Johnny.

Both Chris and I believe in God's power to heal. We both experienced times, especially when we saw Johnny in pain and discomfort, when we longed to see God touch his body and make him whole. Yet we also believe he lived as long as he did because of God's sustaining grace and goodness.

No matter how much we grow with our Lord, we find ourselves confronted again and again with unanswerable questions.

EIGHT

TIME can be both kind and cruel. For us it was a mercy in the passing of days, weeks, and months. Soon, years. We became more and more aware of Johnny's limitations as well as his keen intelligence. But time was cruel to my wife and me in that, as it passed, we sensed a wall rising between us.

I am an enigma to many people and in many ways even to myself. Outwardly I appear to be spontaneously gregarious. Yet, like an iceberg, I tend to keep below the surface far more than appears above even to my closest associates. I am a man of many friends because I travel so widely and meet so many; yet I am a man with few really close friends because I tend to shield myself from time-consuming relationships.

Over the years, when so many who profess to know

Christ's name have permitted their reputations to be marked with questionable morality, I have endeavored to maintain an impeccable reputation. I purposely go to considerable inconvenience, even if it creates an awkward situation, to avoid even the most minute indiscretion with the opposite sex. Chris has never doubted my love, and certainly not my faithfulness.

But man and woman can never be spectators to their own marriage. They must be participants, protagonists and antagonists alike. They may succumb to the abrasions of their relationship and settle for a discordant union. Or together they may build, lesson upon lesson, success against failure, caring and sharing, loving and learning. Under normal circumstances, that is. But the birth of our son imposed stresses rare to any marriage, unknown to most.

Take any husband caught up in the demands of a vital ministry, and a wife who is exceptionally attractive and talented. Normally they would spend much time together, she an important and consistent part of his ministry. But what if circumstances separate them? And even when both are at home, she is engulfed with responsibility, unable many times even to sit down and talk to him.

I tried to be sensitive to my wife's situation, but I seemed to be driven by some kind of relentless energy, never able to settle for the status quo. I couldn't be content to take a pastorate and simply settle into the routine of church life. If the congregation numbered 500, I had to build it to a thousand. If a thousand, then two thousand. Evangelism only amplified my energy. But the incessant pursuit of achievement, however good the motivation, will impose stress on a marriage. Ours had become very vulnerable.

It takes many hours for a husband and wife really to get to know each other—to know when to give, when to receive—and Johnny's coming into our home vastly complicated that process. As Chris became more and more convinced of Johnny's specialness, of his worthiness of the best of a mother's attentions, her concern for him increased rather than diminished. And I was caught up first in a maelstrom of activity centered around an active, growing church, and then in the demands of city-wide evangelism.

"It looks to me like you care an awful lot more for your work than you care for your own wife and son!" Chris snapped at me after one especially trying day with Johnny. "It's exciting, isn't it, meeting people and having them praise what you're doing?"

I went to the telephone and began to dial.

"What are you doing?" Chris demanded.

"Calling to cancel an appointment I had for tonight!" I snapped back.

Chris came to me and forcefully took the phone from my hand. "Speaking of the telephone," she said, "Mrs. Blank called. She wanted to remind you not to forget you're having Sunday dinner with them. She told me how sorry she was I couldn't join you because of Johnny."

I stayed home that evening but we scarcely spoke to each other. I devoted most of the evening to a book.

Chris was anything but a nagging wife. What was happening was that each of us was under daily pressures, mine larger than she realized and hers more debilitating than I realized. Her pressures were out in the open, obvious to both of us. Mine surfaced through a completely unanticipated set of circumstances.

It all began the day she received an anonymous phone call from a woman who asked, "Do you think it's right for you people to raise a cripple and still try to serve a church?"

Before Chris got over the shock of that one, another woman called. "You know you could easily get someone to care for that child. But you live on sympathy. Well, don't expect sympathy from me!"

Then there were calls directly related to me. "He's tearing up our church!" one voice shouted at Chris. Another said, "Oh, sure, he's filling the sanctuary—building up a bunch of supporters to stand with him against those who have been faithful all these years. Why don't you take that kid and get out of town?"

Chris went to the bedroom, closed the door, and asked God for grace to love these people who were making such abusive calls. Then she hurried downstairs and began preparing the best meal she had fixed in over a year.

"Bon appétit!" she sang out when I entered the house.

I took one look at the table, spread for a king, and asked, "Whose birthday is it?"

Chris only smiled, hurried me off to wash up for dinner, and then we all came to the table. We chatted and laughed together through the meal. By prearrangement, after it was finished, Mother Barker cleared the table and went to the kitchen. Chris became tensely serious.

"Something wrong?" I asked.

"There has been," she said. "But I want to help make things right." She told me about the telephone calls. "I didn't realize all you were going through," she said. "Why didn't you tell me?"

"And put a bigger load on your shoulders?"

"It'll be easier for me," she said, "if I know I'm sharing all your experiences. You want to know everything happening to Johnny and he adores you for it. So do I."

We embraced.

Beautifully.

Isn't it strange how we seem to need to go through all of life before we fully grasp the importance of setting wise priorities? I suppose if I had had an eight-to-five job, things might have been a little easier. However, as I so often tell people on my staff, "I'm not looking for anyone who is seeking a forty-hour week but rather for one who is seeking a forty-hour day." The momentum of the ministry, if allowed to dissipate, would be hard to regain. Would these long days involve pulling me farther and farther away from my wife and son?

Or, since God's blessing did seem so obvious on my ministry, should I not expect him to heal Johnny so that mother and son could become part of my activity? "You've got unconfessed sin in your life," one person told us. "If everything is right with you and God, then you can ask for the healing of your son and it will happen immediately." Faith healers came to our area and people urged us to take Johnny. As one reads the miracles of Jesus in the New Testament, one cannot help but think how wonderful it would have been for the Great Physician to reach down and touch Johnny and set him free.

As a matter of fact, I believe that divine healing has occurred in my own life. When I was a child, I fell victim to cholera and hemorrhaged for three days. The doctor told my parents I couldn't possibly live. But, you see, God had a plan for John Haggai. My parents had committed me to the Lord at birth and during that illness they prayed earnestly for the divine touch on my body. They asked for God's will to be done. And God performed his will.

The day after Christmas 1940 I was riding with a friend in an old Model A Ford. We were on a back road. There had been a heavy freeze for several weeks but then the sun came out. We didn't know about the ice under the gravel. Suddenly the car went out of control and turned over. The windshield went over my leg. Just a few inches more and it would have gone over my chest and killed me.

Streptococcus infection set in in the gash in my leg, which the doctor said was the size of half an orange. Thrombosis in my hip was moving to my heart, and the doctors despaired of my survival.

"I think we'd better amputate," one told my parents.

But my father is a man of dauntless faith. "Please wait just a bit longer," he told the doctor. He urged our friends to pray.

"I can't explain it," the physician, an avowed atheist, said a few days later, "unless, like you say, some power other than human intervened."

So I believe in divine healing. But I do not believe that all sickness is the result of personal sin. Sickness has upon it the imprint of the devil's authorship. But a child born with a deformity could not possibly be held accountable for it.

I believe that God heals in five ways. First, he heals through the use of modern medicine. "Every good gift and every perfect gift is from above, and cometh down from the Father of lights, with whom is no variableness, neither shadow of turning" (James 1:17). In developing medication, researchers have simply found what God had already provided. The ingredients for an aspirin tablet were already there. Scientists discovered them, and through the illumination of a beneficent Providence found the proper way of combining them. So if aspirin will relieve a headache, take it. God has given teeth to chew with, so chew with them. God has given eyes to see with, so watch the traffic and don't get run over!

I believe we ought to use medications as necessary, but to understand that it is the prayer of faith that saves the sick. In James 5:14 the writer admonishes us to anoint with oil those who are ill. Oil was used medicinally in biblical times. The man who fell among thieves was rescued by the Good Samaritan who poured oil and wine into his wounds. Those were the two major medicines.

Second, I believe that God heals through the instrumentality of doctors. (Luke, one of the Gospel writers, was a physician.) God grants wisdom to doctors to treat bodies. Every now and then someone will say, "I have a great doctor. He healed me." I know that is not so. Actually, the doctor cut away the obstruction or dealt with the difficulty, whatever it was, so that God's laws of healing could operate. It was God who healed.

Third, I believe that God heals by relieving the stress that may be causing psychosomatic illnesses.

It is a medical fact that many people are suffering from high blood pressure, psychasthenia, peptic and duodenal ulcers, headaches, and many other seemingly physical maladies as a result of stress. When they progress in the Lord and learn to "rejoice" in him, they are healed—because the stress that was creating their problems is relieved.

Fourth, I believe that God heals by direct intervention, as had happened to me twice: as a young child with cholera and after that automobile accident when I was sixteen. In both those instances I believe it was God's will for me to be healed, and he healed me directly. He intervened divinely and sovereignly.

Finally, God heals through the resurrection. That is the only permanent healing, for ultimately we will all die (unless we should still be around at the time of the Lord Jesus Christ's second coming). One of these days our bodies will be changed and "fashioned like unto his glorious body." Then there will be no more sickness, no more pain, no more dying. The tragedy to me is that people so often are interested in the body but not the soul. The body will ultimately go back to the ground from whence it came (unless Jesus Christ comes in the meantime), but the soul will never die.

Many times God has been glorified in the sickness of people. If Fanny Crosby had not been blind, the 8,000 poems and songs that she wrote, blessings to millions of people, might not have been written.

The apostle Paul said, "Trophimus have I left at Miletum *sick*." So the statement that if one has enough faith he or she can be healed is not consistent with the Scriptures. What about the man in John 9 who had been blind for many years? What about the fact that the apostle Paul himself suffered bad eyesight so that to the Galatians he said, "See how large a letter I have written unto you with mine own hand?" And didn't Timothy suffer from a weak stomach, so Paul told him to take a little wine for his stomach's sake?

People who believe that sickness is always the result of personal sin and/or lack of faith nonetheless wear dentures. They don't seem to have an answer for baldness and, ultimately, they all die. Therefore let us "fear not them which kill the body, but are not able to kill the soul: but rather fear him which is able to destroy both soul and body in hell" (Matthew 10:28).

So, of course I believe in healing. The theology of healers is what I question. "We adjure Thee to heal!" the healer challenges the Almighty. I prefer the prayer of Jesus in the garden of Gethsemane. "Nevertheless, not my will but Thine be done!"

If the persistent, trusting prayer of a humble child of God can cause miracles to happen, then surely Johnny would have been lifted out of his infirmity and would be today a vibrant, handsome young man in his late twenties. Prayer for the improvement of one's physical condition is certainly allowed in the Scriptures. Far more often, however, the Scriptures invite us to pray for richness of spirit and wideness of ministry. In these, which are far more important than physical health, Johnny was to abound.

And it was his beautiful mother, sensitive to the will of God and obedient to the Holy Spirit, who would lead him.

NINE

THE WRITING of this book is an experience of pain in many ways. Yet in looking back, I find so few bad memories in contrast with so many good ones. My motivation is to be helpful. I want this book to come into the hands of parents who find themselves confronted by similar situations. For others, Chris's and my experiences may provide preparatory input to help them face problems they do not now foresee. I want to show that God can use anyone, no matter how severely restricted, if that person is willing to be used.

As I said in the Preface, I want this book to be a tribute to my wife Chris. Like a lot of people, she has never accepted herself for what she is really worth. Sometimes I think she consistently does one of the best jobs of negative self-psyche I've ever seen. It's an enigma, really, for Chris is a tremendous person: radiant, attractive, intelligent.

"You've had opportunities to grow and I haven't," she has told me.

At our first church, when the congregation voted me a raise, the chairman said, "We feel Mrs. Haggai ought to get part of the money because she's such a wonderful person and, frankly, she has as great a ministry as the pastor."

Of course, a woman couldn't be self-centered, searching for her own comfort and status, and give herself to the needs of a child the way Chris subsequently did for Johnny. To this day she doesn't realize the significance of the ministry she had with him. Nor does she realize the impact of her life now, as people observe her reaction to his death.

Like almost all young mothers, she anticipated a perfectly normal baby, without so much as a thought of what might otherwise happen. "All things work together for good to them that love God" (Romans 8:28). That promise came blazing into print out of the eternal font of love in the heart of our Lord. "Thus saith the Lord" assures us of absolutes on which we can rest every event and every demand upon our lives. We can be sure of his will for us.

Chris and I are thoroughly convinced that Johnny came to us in the sovereign and loving will of God. Johnny lived a significant life. Significant not just because there is worth in every person, as there surely is, but because the human dimension is so much more vast than most people ever comprehend.

For example, a girl comes into the world with uncomely features. Or a boy never grows beyond sixty inches and is thin and sallow-faced. Another girl faces life with a badly cleft palate. A boy answers the telephone and strangers suppose they are talking to a member of the opposite sex. Dare we relegate such "subspecimens" of humanity to society's shadows?

What then of the handsome brute who is just that— no more than a brute? Or the "beautiful people" for whom life consists of frills and cheap adulations and a future empty of meaning? Yes, beauty really is only skin deep, isn't it? And so is what some people blindly call ugliness.

Johnny was a person of deep and resplendent beauty. And if my telling you about him leads you to seek genuine beauty in other supposedly unfortunate people, then these pages we share together will have been well invested.

Johnny was far more than an object of pity or mercy. In fact, he was more than merely a beautiful person. Johnny became a truly purposeful person. He had a role to fill, a destiny to realize.

Caring for him was not easy. A thousand books could not begin to express the admiration I have for my wife, for the years of patience and self-sacrifice she extended on behalf of our boy.

"Can't we hire somebody to help you?" I often asked, even after Mother Barker came.

"Who'd have the patience?" Chris invariably asked. "For anyone to look after Johnny, that person needs to be taught. I could spend a couple of weeks training such a person. But unless it were a very special person, two weeks would probably be just long enough for that person to decide it was too big a job. I love Johnny with all my heart. I don't know how anyone could look after him who didn't also dearly love him."

Well, thank God, Mother Barker dearly loved him. I remember an incident that happened between her and Johnny before she came to live with us permanently.

Johnny had just passed his second birthday. I was to conduct an evangelistic crusade in Florida and had begged Chris to come with me. She was reluctant to leave Johnny but knew she needed to get away a few days. Mother Barker was all for it.

"Don't you worry one bit," she said. "Johnny and I will get along just fine." She came a couple of days early to learn the routines.

Mother Barker and Johnny took to each other without incident until she began helping Johnny with breakfast. She made the mistake of clicking her dentures, a phenomenon that engulfed Johnny's attention—so much so, he refused to eat. When Mother Barker put food to his mouth he would turn his head away. As he did he showed his teeth.

Well, my mother-in-law is quite a regal lady, but she's also a wonderful sport. She looked at her grandson, smiled wryly, and then let her dentures move a bit in her mouth. Johnny was delighted, demanding encore after encore. Finally, caught up in the festive spirit that had suddenly pervaded the kitchen, Mother Barker performed a feat of such wonder that Johnny was smitten with momentary silence. She took her teeth completely out of her mouth. Johnny began howling with delight. And thereafter, mealtime involved dental escapades, with Mother Barker's two partials more than once ending up on the floor!

Thanks to Mother Barker, Chris and I had a wonderful time in Florida. The crusade drew many people and many made professions of faith in Christ. That many people put a lot of demands on my time but, even so, Chris and I spent more hours alone than had been possible in months at home. I did a lot of thinking. It was good being in evangelism, away from the routines of my church. I thought back to what Dr. Criswell had said. Beyond that, however, I needed to think of Chris, the imposition on her if I were to be gone often—even though for comparatively short periods of time.

We returned home, and I plunged into the work of the church. Johnny continued to grow increasingly alert but was a constant drain on Chris.

By 1956, when our son was five years old, I realized that God's call to me to enter the field of evangelism could be neither ignored nor postponed.

Chris sensed that something was on my mind. "Lots of problems with the church?" she asked.

I smiled, sobered. I would have replied but didn't know what to say.

She needed a few moments to get Johnny to bed. Then she came back to me.

"Chris," I said, "I love and appreciate you more than I can put in words." Then she was the one to keep silent. "You know how tough it is for me as a pastor. A church grows and so do the administrative demands."

"Tell me whatever it is that's on your mind," she urged. "Just tell me."

"Well," I said, "I know I'm not much help in looking after Johnny."

"Except that he brightens up and forgets everything else the minute he hears your footsteps."

"Thanks to you. You could as easily turn him against me. But you're always building me up in his mind, keeping him excited about my work." I was quiet again. Chris waited for me to speak. "I just don't think I belong in the pastorate, Chris. I feel far more comfortable in evangelism."

"If you feel that God wants you to be an evangelist," she said, "then that's what you should do."

"And leave you alone with Johnny?"

"I'm pretty much alone with him now. At least when you're home, you'll be able to give us a lot more of your attention. Now you're gone from early morning to late night with your church responsibilities."

The year before, Mother Barker came with us on a permanent basis. "Now it's two women throwing their lives away," critics gossiped. "That child becomes more of a burden the bigger he gets. If those Haggais had no more sense than the boy has, which can't be much, they'd institutionalize him."

It's incredible how cruel people can be. On the other hand, we probably failed in properly communicating to such folks. Perhaps we should have invited them into our home and let them get to know Johnny as he really was, as we knew him and loved him.

Chris remembers the day, just before I resigned from the church, when one of the women came in on some congregational errand. Johnny had just awakened from a long nap. Suddenly and unpredictably he let out a window-rattling roar. It was the closest he could come to a normal boy's outburst.

"My sakes!" the woman gasped and headed for the door.

Johnny did do things that threw people off when they came to the house. Yet he was no oddity, not really. Not when you knew him well enough to see beyond his corporeal prison, to see the true glow of his boundless spirit.

At the Institute for the Development of Human Potential in Philadelphia, Dr. Glenn Doman, a specialist in cerebral palsy, confirmed our convictions about keeping Johnny. "Children like yours are much better off mentally and emotionally if you keep them at home than if you institutionalize them," he said. "In the first place, it's a rare institution that will give a child anything resembling home-care. Frankly, I don't think Johnny would live. He would succumb to heartbreak if it weren't for the warmth and happiness of his own home." How we cherished those words.

Another specialist told Chris, "If you feel deprived because you can't go out for an evening because of your child, just keep in mind that you wouldn't feel deprived if he were a normal child who came down with some childhood disease. With Johnny it's more permanent, but it's the same thing. That's why your attitude is so important, day by day, toward him and toward yourself." When it came to attitude, Chris was tremendous. I wonder how many women there are who could have weathered those demanding years the way she did.

She kept in close touch with doctors but, as time passed, caring for Johnny made her a kind of specialist in her own right. On more than one occasion doctors would ask her what kind of medication she recommended because she knew Johnny's reaction to many kinds of treatment.

As Johnny grew older it was no longer a matter of simply accepting him. We began to realize that God had given us an exceptional son. Handicapped children are often called exceptional to lessen the hurt on parents, but Johnny was not exceptional in that sense alone. God had sent him to us for a purpose.

I resigned from the church and began an evangelistic ministry. I could write a book on what God did—but as great as some of those experiences were, the highlight of any assignment was always to return to Chris and Johnny. The more it got through to me how devotedly he loved me, how interested he was in my evangelistic efforts, the dearer he became to me.

"He wants you to tell him about what's happened in your meetings," Chris told me.

So I did, perhaps a bit awkwardly at first. But when I saw how intently Johnny listened to what I told him, even though he was still only a small boy, I found myself sharing more and more fully. The older he got, the more boundless became Johnny's capacity for interest and enthusiasm. He had intellectual curiosity. How he accommodated such brightness within the unbroken darkness of such vast discomfort and suffering, I will never be able to understand.

As he grew, like a sapling bent and gnarled, his suffering intensified. He had a tenacious will to live. In actuality, Chris and Mother Barker had to teach him how to survive almost literally from one day, sometimes from one hour, to the next. Our son lived because those two wonderful women made his body function.

Most children learn from watching the conduct of their elders, but Johnny couldn't mimic us. Everything he did had to be adapted to his particular situation. Chewing. Swallowing. By trial and error, Chris laboriously taught him how. He was so grateful when he had achieved some simple function that gratitude would well up in his eyes.

We seldom thought of him as an abnormal child, but as a special child. We simply didn't measure him in the way others measure handicapped youngsters. One of life's most enriching dimensions is learning to discover what real personhood is, and someone like Johnny can really teach that lesson. Stripped of the usual physical attributes, unable to communicate normally, forced to settle for nearly zero rapport with so many of the people he met, Johnny learned how to enrich people inwardly. We looked past his deformity, his limitation—the "deep" in us reaching out to the "deep" in him.

I would return from a crusade, for example, to find Johnny all cleaned up and waiting. When I entered the room, he would squeal with delight. It was different, of course, than a normal father greeting a normal child, but not less endearing. Even then, young as he was, I began a communication with him that became very meaningful in the years ahead. He drank in every word, eyes wide, body held in tense silence. The older he got, the more I saw him as as real a person as I met anywhere. That's why it didn't anger me when people lacked the capacity to understand him. They were as handicapped as he was (in some instances, perhaps even more handicapped).

Johnny's condition was never an embarrassment to me. As far as I was concerned, anyone who wouldn't accept my son didn't really accept me either. I can't remember being defensive about him at all. My only concern was that people would think him something less than he was and then treat him demeaningly. It was the "house" in which Johnny lived that was in shambles. The occupant of the house was just fine.

That's why, as he got older, I began to suggest that he and Chris go along to some of the crusades. My wife was quite timid about the idea at first, but Johnny was ready and eager. So they came occasionally. It was difficult for Chris, not having the special equipment we had arranged at home, but she managed. And I was so glad to have them with me.

People can be wonderful. Many times when Johnny was along for a crusade, people made a definite point of meeting him. Johnny relished that. He was so real inside, he just naturally reached out to people. Of course there were times when Chris realized that Johnny's presence made others uncomfortable. If she and Johnny were at a crusade, for example, and such individuals happened to be about, she would turn his wheelchair away from them or push it over to a remote corner.

Many people had a tendency to talk down to Johnny, a situation he loathed. But there were happy exceptions. Newscaster Paul Harvey has been a close friend of the family for many years, and frequently gives news bits about our Third World ministry on his broadcasts. Paul was good to Johnny.

So was Bob Pierce, founder of World Vision. "Hey, Buddy," Bob would say in his characteristic manner, "I'm counting on you to pray for me when I go to Korea next month." Johnny would have gladly listened all day to Bob reporting on experiences overseas.

The crusade ministry continued to grow, and I couldn't begin to accept all the invitations. When a crusade invitation came from Honolulu, Chris agreed to bring Johnny and come with me. He fell in love with Hawaii. He, his mother, and Mother Barker spent hours on Waikiki, exploring the gardens and quiet walkways.

One night we took him to an outdoor restaurant overlooking the beach. A group of singers were entertaining with traditional Hawaiian melodies. The restaurant was illuminated with torches. We didn't notice how irritated a woman at a nearby table was until she leaped to her feet and stormed toward us. "Haven't you got your nerve," she thundered, "bringing that miserable child out in public when some of us would like to have a decent meal?" She left the restaurant.

I felt sorry for that woman, wealthy, perhaps, with this world's goods. I suppose she had some prestige, at least in her small circle. But how little she knew of life. How empty she must have been. I felt love and pity for her, and for many others like her.

Sometimes people, feeling sorry for our son, slipped money into his pocket. On occasion we found as much as a dollar in coins when we took off his coat. We used to tease him about this. "One of these days we'll have to put a tin cup in your hand and let you sit on the street," Chris said.

Johnny laughed uproariously. He thrived on that kind of candor and teasing.

Children took a special interest in him and, children being as they are, would ask blunt questions about him. "What's the matter with him? Was he in an accident?"

Chris had immaculate tact in handling such situations. She might ask, "Do you know what polio is?" (It was the days before Salk vaccine.) "Johnny's problem is similar to those who have had very bad cases of polio."

She never hedged at questions. If a stranger asked, she simply told Johnny's story. Often such an opportunity opened up a chance to witness. Johnny might be quite fretful and tired, but whenever he heard his mother telling someone about him, he became very quiet. He seemed to relish hearing his own story.

Witness really means just being a tool in the Holy Spirit's hands. If we are yielded, if we want Christ first in our lives, then the Holy Spirit will lead us to witnessing opportunities. Chris certainly found it so.

For example, one day the power company sent a new man to read the meter at our house.

"Lovely day, isn't it?" Chris greeted, letting him in.

"Depends on how you look at it," he grumbled.

"Oh," my wife countered, "the Bible says 'This is the day that the Lord has made. Let us rejoice and be glad in it.' "

The meter man stopped, looked at his order sheet, and then snapped, "You're a preacher's wife. Got a free house and everything. They probably give your husband a car and pay for the gas. People like you don't know what it's like to have it tough."

Chris smiled and showed him where to find the meter.

When he came back he headed straight for the door, but Chris intercepted him. "Would you mind stepping into the other room a minute?" she asked. "I'd like you to meet our son." The young man reluctantly followed.

There lay Johnny, sprawled out on his special bed, his big dark eyes wide with greeting, a smile broad upon his face.

"Johnny," Chris said, "this is our meter man. Young man, I would like you to meet Johnny."

That afternoon the meter man went to Georgetown, Kentucky. While there, visiting friends, he told them about the experience with Johnny and what an impact it had made upon his spiritually. The friends he was visiting lived next door to a couple who had a daughter with cerebral palsy. They were extremely bitter about their daughter's condition. After the meter man left, his friends told their neighbors the story of Chris's poise and charm and the unusual experience the meter man had with Johnny. The parents of the cerebral palsied daughter were so impressed that they went to a local church that very night and were both converted. They became active members of the church.

Another time the phone rang. A woman called saying she understood we had purchased a new refrigerator similar to one she was thinking of buying. Could she come over and see it? As cordially as she could,

Chris told the woman to come. She was feeding Johnny when the stranger arrived and told her she needed to continue but for her to look at the refrigerator and feel free to ask any questions. The woman apparently knew nothing about Johnny and became very curious and then quite fascinated. She almost forgot the real purpose of her visit.

"May I pour you a cup of coffee?" Chris asked.

"I don't want to bother you."

"No bother," Chris said pleasantly, as she went and poured a cup.

Then the woman asked, "How do you ever cope with it?"

"With Johnny?" Chris gave Johnny a loving pinch on the cheek. "He's a darling!"

Just then Johnny had some of his chronic digestive difficulty. Chris hurried to make him comfortable.

"He must take hours of your day," the visitor said.

"God permits things for a purpose in our lives," Chris told her. "If I'm faithful, God will bless me for that faithfulness. If I refuse to accept what God permits, I'll be the loser."

Chris attended to Johnny for a few moments. Then, noticing how silent the woman had become, she turned to her and found her at the point of tears. "My husband died six months ago of a heart attack," the visitor said. "I've been blaming God for taking my husband away from me."

The Lord permitted Chris to share deeply from her experiences and from the Bible what she had learned about acceptance and confidence in faith—a testimony that helped the unexpected visitor to commit her life to Christ and become an active, witnessing Christian.

TEN

O F THE MANY LESSONS life has taught me, none stands out more than this: God allows no need in our lives for which he does not provide adequate supply. Our importunity, as someone has said, becomes God's opportunity. It is a plain promise of Scripture. "My God shall supply all your needs, according to his riches in glory, through Christ Jesus." In the book of Philippians the apostle Paul stated that promise of God's supply after commenting upon the Philippians' faithfulness in honoring God through their stewardship. Receiving from God is only part of a two-way street. We reciprocate by the outflow of ourselves, of our means, to him.

Certainly Chris's mother proved to be one of God's special provisions for our family. Dear Mother

Barker! She lives with us yet, her voice a sound of joy each morning. Witty. Resourceful. In her insights, her understanding, since Day One, she could be consistently counted upon to brighten a dull day or add a touch of warmth and strength when things became difficult.

God will surely have a place in heaven for every mother who, having reared her own family, willingly assumes the responsibility of another. To move into a household and share the task of looking after Johnny equaled the care of many youngsters. You didn't get Johnny up in the morning, see him clothed and fed, and then send him off to school. You didn't fix him a sandwich, pour a glass of milk, and send him outside to play. You watched him constantly. Many many times Johnny would have choked and died, were it not for that constant surveillance.

During those early years, Mother Barker fed, bathed, dressed, and then entertained our son between meals. Because of his chronic problems with improper digestion, not one day in his lifetime did he successfully keep down all the food he ate. Often he lost an entire meal. He lived with that condition, but he never accepted it. Always, whenever it happened, hurt and disappointment came to his eyes.

"There now, Johnny," Mother Barker inevitably comforted, "just don't you worry. We'll take care of it."

She would wipe away the mess, take off his soiled clothes, clean him up again. And all the time she quietly reassured him, turning his mind to diversions around him or to anticipated pleasantries of the day. Then, to salve his frustration, she would bring out something bright for him to put on. After that, as

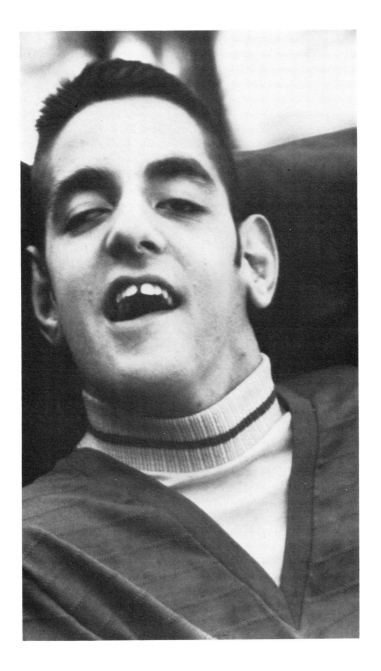

Johnny's warm smile touched hearts wherever he went.

Chris and Johnny (four months old) on the steps of our Chattanooga, Tennessee, pastorium.

Christmas 1953, in Chattanooga. Johnny, three years old.

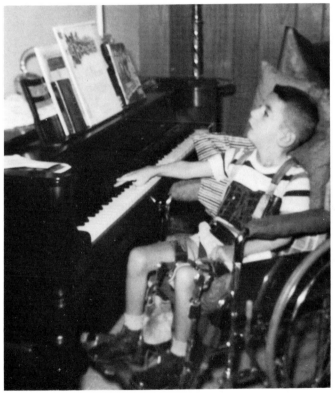

Johnny's fifth birthday, Louisville, Kentucky, 1955.

Six-year-old Johnny was fascinated by the piano. He shared his mother's love for music.

Young Nak Presbyterian Church in Seoul, Korea (world's largest Presbyterian Church), 1970. Associate pastor (now senior minister) Dr. Cho-Choon Park interpreting.

Jakarta, Indonesia, November 1967. Adults with me, from left to right: associate pastor Dr. Henky Tan, director Gay Juban, associate Felix Snipes.

The annual banquet of Haggai Institute, January 24, 1975. At Chris's left is Dr. Chandu Ray, the Institute's faculty anchorman who was formerly an Anglican bishop in Karachi, Pakistan.

*Christmas 1972 at Stone Mountain, Georgia. Johnny,
twenty-two years old.*

May 1975: Chris and I fly around the world on an information survey for the Haggai Institute.

Chris and Johnny looking through French doors to the patio, just a few days before Johnny's Homegoing.

though nothing had happened, she quietly helped him finish his food.

"You have no idea how much your help means to us," I often told her.

"I love Johnny," would be her reply. And she meant it. He loved her too.

The nature of our son's needs imposed a communal lifestyle upon us all, with Johnny the hub of the total household day. We related to each other through him. That could have invited all kinds of tensions, but it didn't—and Mother Barker was certainly one of the significant reasons.

No wonder Johnny took to her. Whether she's in church, walking through a park, or in some kind of social gathering, children seem instinctively drawn to her. The minister of education at our church in Atlanta calls her "the darling of the senior citizens." She surrounded her grandson with her natural vivacity.

It was Mother Barker who introduced Johnny to the typewriter. Carefully, she took his little hand, selected the pointing finger for him, and showed him how to press the keys. For an hour at a time he would sit trying to type. "Write a letter to Grandma," Mother Barker encouraged him, and he typed all the harder.

Early in life Johnny developed an insatiable curiosity. Any strange sound caught his attention and held it until he determined the cause. He quickly detected new things brought into the room, a vase of flowers, a striking picture, bright clothes.

Mother Barker delighted in dressing him up in his finest array. Her pleasure was exceeded only by

Johnny's when she held him up to a mirror. "Well, there," she would tell him, "aren't you just the handsomest little fellow in town?" To which Johnny gurgled with delight.

We once had a noisy furnace, and Johnny began noticing every time it flipped on and off. "That's the furnace, down in the basement," Mother Barker told him. "It keeps us warm." She never should have brought up the subject, for Johnny couldn't settle for any mere verbal explanation. He had to see it. He had to see that furnace right now! So Mother Barker picked him up, husky though he had become, and carried him down the basement steps.

Now it so happened that Johnny had never been in so dark and strange a place before, nor had his eyes ever come upon such a monstrous object as a furnace. He began to howl at the top of his lungs. At the first sound of his outcry, Mother Barker thought he might be registering delight over what he saw. But he quickly put such a thought out of her mind, as he wiggled and squirmed and lurched his body back toward the stairs. He had had enough of dark places and strange objects, and it took a long time before he would again venture into such unknowns.

I have great love and admiration for my own parents, about whom I'll go into more detail later. But I never feel guilty comparing my wife's mother with my own. Mother Barker was an entity unto herself. I not only accepted her, I cherished her. She earned and sustained a place in our family as secure as if she had always been part of the household. Her misgivings about me years before, when her daughter showed her my photograph in the Moody Bible Institute annual, gave way to great warmth. She never told me so, not in so many words, but I like to think I became her favorite preacher.

She loves her Bible, and we occasionally discuss various passages. She has a particular yen for controversial subjects. For example, once she came to me with her Bible open to the eleventh chapter of Luke and asked, "What does Jesus mean here when he says 'Woe unto you also, ye lawyers!'?" She is a resolute politician, a committed Republican. Watergate devastated her political morale because she trusted all Republicans as fervently as she mistrusted all Democrats.

She loves baseball. Hank Aaron never had a more loyal fan while he played for our Atlanta Braves. If she turned on television and saw her team losing, however—no matter how action-packed and interesting the game might be—she would promptly push the *off* button.

She's a total, all-around, gracious, and fascinating person. I wish she could sit down beside every lonely person in our country and tell him how beautiful life can be in its golden years. And tell them how to make it so. How to become more valuable—so needed, yet so unobtrusive that those younger want you because they need you, because they treasure your counsel and esteem you as a person.

Many times when the load became heavy, when Johnny had difficult days, Mother Barker's resources stemmed from her dependence upon the Lord. Yet she was no starry-eyed religionist, no legalist living under a proud canopy of I-do-but-you-don't.

We're Southern Baptists, and Southern Baptists

are accused of expecting a place in heaven to be cordoned off just for them (although, in all fairness, Southern Baptists have continued to identify more and more with the total evangelical community in recent years). My mother-in-law has always been first and foremost a Christian, and second a member of a denomination.

But in addition to that, she possesses the virtue of seeing herself as a human being, and as such, she was so good for Johnny. They bantered back and forth. She realized just how far to carry a joke, how much to tease until he had had enough.

Yet she was no child's easy touch. With the passing of time, as Chris increased her determination to rear our son as a normal person, it became necessary at times to apply the discipline all children must receive if they are to develop proper patterns of conduct. Chris believed that discipline, properly administered, could be a parent's highest expression of love. Discipline, so administered, gave a child the security and sense of self-value so necessary to a well-balanced life. Mother Barker shared that conviction to the full.

Grandparents can be counterproductive, by providing grandchildren with opportunities to conduct themselves in a manner alien to their parents' wishes. My mother-in-law had no part of that. She may have disagreed with her daughter at times, but she didn't undermine her.

The older he got, the more beautiful became Johnny's personality. We loved him for it. But he also had a will of steel. "Why did the Lord have to give me two cut from the same cloth?" Chris chided me one day.

For the most part, though, Johnny was consistently tolerant, whatever the circumstances. In fact, Mother Barker says she never saw her grandson display his wrath until the last year of his life. He could become angry, however, even though covertly, and Chris made it a strict point never to give in to him under such circumstances.

I must admit, however, that I was just the contrary. I found it very difficult to be firm with my son. I was the kind who would romp with him, tell him stories, recount experiences I had had, but stand helpless if he became fretful. "Chris, will you come see what Johnny wants?" was one of my more frequent expressions.

One summer Homer Rodeheaver invited us to be his house guests at Winona Lake, Indiana. Having been Billy Sunday's songleader for so many years, Mr. Rodeheaver took a special interest in evangelists and spent many hours searching out my mind and heart as well as sharing from his own experience.

One afternoon Chris and I took Johnny for a stroll along the beach and came to the private swimming area maintained by the Winona Lake Bible Conference. Even though the water was quite cold, Johnny wanted to go swimming. And, of course, he wanted to go right then. After all, he had me along as fortification against a likely maternal refusal.

"No, Johnny," his mother told him, "today we are just going to enjoy looking at the water, not swimming in it."

Johnny turned immediately to me.

"She's right, Buddy," I told him, but not with enough firmness to convince him the cause was lost. He threw himself against his chair and began to protest.

"No, Johnny," I reprimanded him, but gently. He became all the more adamant.

Whereupon, to the amazement of both Johnny and his mother—and to myself as well—I swept him out of the wheelchair, turned him across my lap, and gave him a lively spanking.

"After this, ol' Buddy," I told him calmly but firmly, "when you're told something, that's the way it's to be." Johnny was an exemplary child for the remainder of that day.

It meant much to have a household united in opinion about the management of our son. And particularly to enjoy the special cooperation of Mother Barker, a woman of strong personal opinion, yet big enough to subordinate herself. She did it graciously and, in so doing, contributed a positive influence to the development of her grandson's personality and character.

She possessed exactly the qualities needed to care for and to influence him. She complimented him for all his good points. She demonstrated compassion when he suffered, always trying to help him see a silver lining through the clouds looming above him. She was a real person to Johnny and he to her. How much more tolerable and productive life on this planet would be if the human race had more like her.

ELEVEN

WHEN we took Johnny to Philadelphia Institute for the Development of Human Potential, he had a session with Dr. Eugene Spitz, head of the University of Pennsylvania Medical School's Department of Neurosurgery. "Your son has an exceptionally fine mind," Dr. Spitz said. "Unfortunately, we have no methods devised for giving an IQ test to someone in his situation. But were we to do so, I have no question but that he would have a rating in the junior-genius or genius class." That would be somewhere between 160 or 170, I believe.

Of course, not only could Johnny not take intelligence tests, but neither could we give him the kind of toys that would provide windows to his mind.

I mentioned earlier our friendly neighbor, Ollie Merchant. Mr. Merchant took special pains to show Johnny warm attention, a human grace to which he always responded with beaming appreciation. Mr. Merchant mowed his lawn every Saturday afternoon, and Chris would roll Johnny outside so he could watch.

Mr. Merchant began leaving a little spot of grass each Saturday under a shade tree where Johnny could first sit and watch and then, subsequently, help push the mower a bit. I think Mr. Merchant purposely let the machine run out of fuel occasionally so Johnny could observe him go through the routine of refueling and starting it. If only Johnny could have pulled that starter cord himself.

Johnny also became assistant chef when Mr. Merchant grilled steaks. "I've got some trimming to do on this hedge around the house," our neighbor would tell Johnny, as casually as he would tell anyone. "Please watch those steaks. If the fire gets up too high, call me."

Johnny riveted his eye onto the grill. The moment the fire began to leap above the meat, he called out at the top of his voice, "Yeah!"

"Thanks, Johnny!" Mr. Merchant would call back, coming hurriedly.

Johnny was intrigued by anything and everything mechanical and noisy. Gasoline pumps, for example, fascinated him. When a mechanic worked on our car, if we could possibly arrange it we permitted Johnny to watch. If that boy had just one steady hand, capable of holding a screwdriver and pliers, I suppose he would have tried to take apart and reassemble every gadget in our house.

I like to think that penchant simply validated him as an authentic Haggai. My brother Ted, for example, is a sophisticated gadgeteer. Ted invented the demodulator, which reportedly helped save many American lives during the Vietnam conflict. As one of five senior scientists at Hughes Aircraft, Ted headed the team that developed Syncom, the communications satellite that makes possible instantaneous communication of television signals to any place on earth. Ted was awarded the L. A. Hyland Patent Award for Scientific Achievement. I imagine that some of the dynamic genetics it took to produce a Ted Haggai may have structured our son's inert capability.

While I'm on the subject of our family tree—because I think it may further help you understand Johnny—let me tell you a bit about my younger brother, Tom. He's what I call a minister to the marketplace. "If people won't come to church," Tom avows, "then we must take the church to the people." Tom is chairman of the board of IGA. He is much sought after as a speaker. He was awarded the rare and coveted Silver Buffalo award, the Scouts' highest honor (given to such men as Dwight Eisenhower, Bernard Baruch, and Douglas MacArthur). Tom so resembles me in appearance, by the way, that when he first visited us, Johnny puzzled long over the similarity. Even our voices are markedly similar, except Tom has a distinct southern accent.

But back to our son's fascination for things mechanical. The summer we visited Homer Rodeheaver, our host took a special liking to Johnny. He expanded his hospitality to provide activities calculated to widen the eye of any adventure-prone youngster.

"Say!" he exclaimed one afternoon. "I have an idea, Johnny. See what you think about it. We've got that big lake out there. I understand you like water. Well, it so happens I own the fastest speedboat on Winona Lake. How about taking a ride?"

"Yeah!" Johnny responded, with the full crescendo of both his lungs.

"But, of course, if you don't care to go," Homer teased.

"Yeah!" our son assured him, more loudly than before. So we wheeled Johnny out to dockside as our host checked the fuel supply and warmed up the engine.

Anyone who remembers Homer Rodeheaver knows how he loved to sing. He could take a simple gospel song and treat it like an operatic finale. In his day, you know, he set America to singing "Brighten the Corner." Our visit was soon after he had composed music for Dr. Oswald Smith's lovely lyrics, "Then Jesus Came." So, as we moved away from shore, the man who had directed vast choirs and performed for presidents and kings began singing:

> *One sat alone beside the highway begging.*
> *His eyes were blind, the light he could not see.*
> *He clutched his rags and shivered in the shadows,*
> *Then Jesus came and bade his darkness flee.*

Johnny listened entranced. He loved that song and absolutely no one could sing it the way Homer Rodeheaver did, with or without accompaniment. Moving into the refrain, as he also accelerated the boat motor, the famed musician pulled out all the stops:

> *When Jesus comes, the tempter's power is broken.*
> *When Jesus comes, the tears are wiped away.*
> *He takes the gloom and fills the heart with glory.*
> *For all is changed when Jesus comes to stay.*

Under any other circumstances, our son would have listened enrapt to the entire rendition. But the sudden roar of acceleration turned his eyes back to the big motor as it tested its full strength against the placid surface of the lake. For Johnny this was a new wonder under the sun. It was mechanical. It demonstrated power. It overwhelmed him. And it made a delightful noise!

It was, in fact, Johnny's initial sensitivity both to pleasure and the things he didn't like that helped us recognize his intelligence. Chris had more sessions with doctors than I did, and she remembers a time when a doctor tried to get us to institutionalize Johnny.

"But when we go for a ride," Chris told him, "he recognizes streets and the directions we're going."

"Perhaps you only think so," the doctor said.

"But if we turn and head toward home, and he doesn't want to go, he becomes very fretful," she added. "On the other hand, he loves the park near our house, possibly because he associates that with the tennis courts where his grandfather beats his father in tennis. If he sees us driving in that direction, his eyes light up and he does his best to impress upon us how pleased he is."

The doctor only shook his head, convinced that

Chris was just unwilling to face the inclement facts about her child.

Love, you know, like the meandering of a river, seeks out many courses. No two rivers flow the same. Neither do any two mothers respond identically to their offspring. It is my hope that telling Johnny's story, with its inevitable glimpses of his mother's character and commitment, will help others see that our God is the great Designer. He has a plan for every human being. A girl need not become Miss America, nor a boy the athlete of the century, to affirm God's handiwork. What we do with a newborn baby the Creator places into our custody counts just as much.

Many of the social problems facing our country would be quickly resolved if parents could only realize that they are, in many respects, potters. The children they bring into the world are moldable clay. But mental growth requires guidance, stimulation, and encouragement.

Chris often wished that Johnny might have had more playmates as a child. Some neighbor children, the one little girl especially, got to know him. But none ever spent enough time with him to catch the knack of understanding his ways. Consequently, our son grew up in an adult world. In a sense, he bypassed childhood.

I'm sure no family ever drew a handicapped child more into the center of their lives than we did. It was no token involvement, believe me. We kept him informed, solicited his opinion, involved him in decision making. As a result he reacted more and more distinctly to all that happened.

Partly because he could not talk, he developed a

strong talent for listening. He had a memory like a computer. Days later, when something came up in a conversation, he might pose questions. The answer, we would ultimately discover, lay in a brief statement he had heard days before.

When I went into evangelism I formed an association with a board of directors. I was paid a modest salary, received travel and accommodations expenses, but any excess funds from the crusades went into the organization's treasury. I've always believed in the counsel of a good board. There is a danger, you know, that a person who forms his own organization will try to surround himself with "yes" men. When I was in evangelism I had an excellent board of competent, clear-thinking men. And for our present Haggai Institute ministry, one of the directors said, "I have been on some of America's leading boards, both sacred and secular, and I don't believe there is a board anywhere comparable to that group of men who serve as directors for this organization." I had to agree. I listen to those men because I so completely trust their competence.

Johnny was scarcely an adolescent when I realized how interested he was in the functions of our board (then the board governing the evangelistic crusades). He would sit by the hour and listen as I told him what went on in board meetings. He took a keen interest in finances and wanted me to go into detail about economics, especially when we later inaugurated our training program for Third World leaders.

When I was in evangelism, as with our present Third World ministry, we were not without problems. Well, let me tell you, Johnny could read a person's mood. He could sense when there was some unusual pressure and he always wanted to know about it. He would become so distraught at times you'd think he was responsible for the current difficulty. I used to kid him and say, "You know, Johnny, there's a book you should read. It's called *How to Win Over Worry*. I forget the name of the author." That always brought a chuckle, even in his dourest moods.

So I read portions of my book to him. As he got older he attended seminars where I gave lectures based on the book. I like to think my *How to Win Over Worry* had something to do with the way he was able to accept his lot in life so well.

The older he got, the more Johnny loved to travel— whether to the grocery store or across the world. I wish we could have taken him more places. After every trip you could see how his thinking had widened. I wonder if he ever forgot a place he visited or a person he met. He had an uncanny knack for remembering landmarks. He often remembered roads we had forgotten. It was a familiar occurrence on a trip for me to ask, "Do we turn at this road, Johnny, or go straight ahead?" Again and again Johnny led the right way.

He was just ten when we moved to Atlanta, where he lived for the remainder of his short life, and I remember one time taking him on some errand. I was preoccupied with other things and, though I found the place I was going without difficulty, I became completely confused on directions as we headed back.

"Umn!" Johnny protested all of a sudden.

"What's the matter, Buddy?" I asked. "Did I turn the wrong way?"

"Yeah," Johnny said.

So I circled the block and got back onto the main thoroughfare from which I had turned. "Is the street we turn on up ahead?" I asked.

"Yeah," Johnny replied, with a kind of dry humor as though he were giving me a friendly put-down for not knowing the way. We drove along for two or three blocks. Then Johnny abruptly called out, "Yeah!" There was the main street just up ahead.

"Do I go to the left?" I asked. I was really confused.

"Umn!" Johnny replied. So when I reached the intersection, I turned to the right. "Yeah," Johnny said softly. Like a professional navigator, my ten-year-old son guided his confused father safely home.

On our first trip to Hawaii I rented a Hertz convertible and took him on a tour of Waikiki. Johnny was absolutely ecstatic. He called out greetings to every person he saw.

He developed a keen interest in politics and wanted to vote as he grew older. We tried to figure a way but couldn't. Johnny was understanding, but very frustrated.

When he was midway into his teens we arranged one of the telephone extensions so he could talk with the help of his mother or grandmother. I called him frequently, and there were others who also mastered the knack of conversing with him. Someone needed to be right on hand whenever his telephone rang because he wanted to get to it immediately.

"It's a good thing you don't work down at our office," I chided him. "Our telephone bill is big enough now. If you were around, we'd probably have calls to places all over the world."

"Yeah," Johnny agreed, grinning broadly.

Chris and I feel that one of the surest signs of our son's full intelligence lay in the way he mastered the art—for it surely was an art—of accepting himself. As I've said before, he had a twenty-second delay in response. When it may have seemed he didn't understand, it was simply a matter of his trying to program his mind so he could respond. The more relaxed he was, the less time it took him to program. With those of us at home, and particularly with Chris, his response was almost instant at times.

We naturally thought of sending him some place to school, and on one of my crusades I heard about an institution that seemed uniquely suitable to Johnny's situation. Instead of institutionalizing him it would be like going to a private school. He would come home for the holidays and spend the summers with us. It looked like a real answer.

It so happened that I was to have a crusade a few months later in that very city, so Chris and Mother Barker decided to bring Johnny and come down for the last days on the schedule. Johnny responded to that prospect with pure elation—until Chris said, "We're going a day early, Johnny, to investigate a school."

He became instantly sober and began to pout.

"But your father has already been to this school," she responded. "The man in charge said you can go right in with the other children."

Chris stopped at the school and left Johnny with other children while she and her mother took a forty-five minute tour around the campus. They were scarcely out of sight when Johnny began to cry as though his heart would break. He continued crying until they returned.

"Your son would never survive here," the supervisor told Chris.

Later, when we did take him to the Institute for the Development of Human Potential in Philadelphia, they had a strict policy prohibiting parents from seeing their handicapped children during the initial two months. By the second day, however, Johnny was so brokenhearted that Chris was asked to come for him. "We can't get through to him at all," one of the staff workers said. "We can't even get him to eat."

It troubled Chris. She wanted the best for Johnny. Since she had tried so hard not to pamper him, why couldn't he be gone for periods of time now as he grew older?

"Occasionally we meet a rare child like this," one of the therapists comforted Chris. "Because of his intelligence, he realizes how precarious his situation is. He has come to trust you, to know he will be properly cared for when he has physical difficulty. So he naturally fears what the outcome could be in the care of strangers, even though he knows they may be competent. In the case of your son, there is no question but that he belongs at home."

Yet we have no feelings of guilt about how we handled our son. We did the very best for him. And in the meaningful aspects of life, he couldn't have had better training than his own mother gave him. Yet when I think of my brothers Ted and Tom, and of the opportunities God has given me for service, I can only wonder what kind of potential lay in Johnny's brain like unmined gold.

"Johnny," I told him once, "when we get to heaven, please don't tell us how stupid we've been!"

"I think it was a stroke of Satan," I said to Chris once, "bringing Johnny into the world in his condition. Satan thought he could nullify our effectiveness for Christian service." But if so, how wrong Satan was.

TWELVE

I N MY WORK as a pastor and evangelist I have frequently met people who evidenced sincerity and validity as Christians, yet who couldn't point to a time and place of conversion. I emphasized evangelism in my pastoral ministry. Evangelism forms the core of Haggai Institute in Singapore and of the widening circles of outreach from that ministry. I believe, of course, in the need for growth in the Christian life. But, in the Christian experience, birth predates life, and growth occurs only when life has occurred.

In my evangelistic crusades I structured my messages to appeal to reason, to the human will, rather than simply to emotions. As time passed, as Johnny heard more and more of my preaching, Chris and I assumed that the enthusiasm he demonstrated stemmed from his own personal relationship to Jesus Christ. As you now understand, so much went on inside Johnny's mind that we could only assume.

What was actually happening, however, was that we—like so many well-intentioned parents—assumed too much. No child, however exemplary or in whatever manner he or she has been influenced, becomes a Christian by osmosis. Whether or not the exact moment can be remembered, every person—if he or she is to be numbered in God's family—must have at some time experienced that greatest of all miracles, new birth.

"You must be born again," Jesus said.

Though Johnny loved preaching, he became more intensely involved at the close of each service when I gave the invitation for people to publicly acknowledge their acceptance of Christ. Such a look of wonder came to his eyes, Chris told me, and she especially remembered the time she first detected tears. She, too, wept to think that our son nurtured such an awareness of the spiritual crisis transpiring in people's lives.

As years passed, although Chris took Johnny to the crusades as often as possible, they could by no means attend all of them. So, when I returned from any such mission, Johnny wanted an immediate report.

"Buddy," I often told him, "God answered our prayers again. I really appreciate the way you stand behind me." I will always remember the look in Johnny's eyes on such occasions. And the blindness in our own hearts.

For, while he rejoiced in the increasing evidence of God's blessing on the meetings, there were telltale evidences of spiritual unrest in his own heart, evidences we ought to have recognized.

He grew fitful at the sound of some hymns, especially hymns of invitation such as "Just As I Am." He became so emotionally upset if I preached a sermon on hell that Chris deliberately avoided bringing him to such meetings. He was at that time only a boy of eight, yet many people, many outstanding Christians, have come to Christ by the time they reached that age.

Understandably, Johnny didn't like sermons on death. He never did, as long as he lived. We presumed his aversion to sermons on hell stemmed from his concern for the lost, his reluctance to think of anyone perishing when God had so adequately provided salvation in Christ. And too, death hovered constantly nearby him, like a foreboding specter. So the months passed without our realizing the full dimensions of our son's spiritual thinking.

The following summer I conducted a crusade in Mississippi and urged Chris and Johnny to attend. He had had several good weeks, but had been confined at home for a long time. So Chris agreed to come. It was a difficult crusade because of the heat and humidity, but large crowds attended and God blessed the preaching with thrilling responses night after night.

Johnny had never seemed more intent. Nor more nervous.

"I almost wonder if we should have brought him," Chris told me one night. "He loves the music and sermons but gets so restless."

The crusade was held in a football stadium, an

ideal setting in Johnny's estimation. He felt more at ease outdoors, more free to express himself. But that following night, after Chris spoke to me, he seemed particularly restless. The moment I began to give the invitation, he lurched forward in his wheelchair. He wore braces so he could keep his body reasonably erect, and one of the braces was anchored to his shoe. When he wanted to be moved, he often clicked the metal brace against the footplate of his chair. He clicked loudly that night.

Chris looked at him and smiled, but there was no smile on Johnny's face. Anguish burned like a subdued flame in his eyes. His lips drew taut. Perspiration stood out on his forehead. Chris had never seen anything quite like it before. Was he on the verge of a seizure? When she questioned Johnny, however, he made it clear that something else was happening.

At that moment, an awareness dawned in my wife's heart. *Heavenly Father*, she prayed silently, *could it be that Johnny has never really experienced a living faith?* The question seemed both pertinent and preposterous. Yet when a person came to our crusade, our first concern was not that person's background. Did he come from a Christian home? Did he attend a good church? What did he think about the Bible? No, our concern was whether or not that person has been born again. So why make an exception with our own son?

"Johnny," Chris whispered, "do you want to go forward like the others?"

"Yeah!" he blurted.

Now it was Chris who felt ill at ease. She looked nervously about, wondering what people might think

—while Johnny continued clicking the brace against his chair more impetuously and loudly.

"That's wonderful," Chris told him, "but let's wait until we get home. I'll take you to our pastor and we'll talk to him. I'm sure he'll arrange for you to go forward in our church, where you can give your heart to Jesus. Won't that be better?"

Johnny didn't answer. But his hair grew wet from perspiration. He became as drenched, in fact, as if he were sitting in a light rain.

Chris wanted to oblige him but hesitated in the realization that both of us consciously avoided making any show whatever of our son. If he were to be pushed to the front of the field with the other inquirers, critics might say that we had planned it, that we had waited for a strategic moment to exploit his pathetic disability. So she didn't push him forward.

Disappointment spread like a cloud across Johnny's countenance as the time came for the benediction. Chris wheeled him off to one side and had a long talk with him, carefully explaining what was involved, the meaning of faith, the fact of sin.

"The Bible tells us, 'all have sinned and come short of the glory of God,'" she said, "just as Daddy so often tells people in his sermons. I have sinned. That's why I opened my heart to the Lord Jesus as a girl. You have sinned, too. Like when you get so angry sometimes. When you're rebellious and don't want to do what we ask you to do."

Wide-eyed, Johnny drank in every word. Unquestionably, the Holy Spirit was working in his heart. But the Holy Spirit was at work in his mother's heart too. Why were we so concerned about what people might say? Was it right for me to invite others to make a public profession of faith in Christ but deny our own child?

When we got back to the motel I could see how troubled Johnny was. I didn't say anything until Chris had put him to bed. Then she explained what had happened. "What shall I do?" she asked. "People know Johnny's at the meetings. They know he's your son. If I push the wheelchair to the front, won't it make too much of a spectacle?"

"We want him to have as many normal experiences as possible," I told her. Yet I was as perplexed as she was, as disinclined to approve Johnny's request.

The next night was the closing night of the crusade. Johnny could hardly wait to get to the stadium, to join the crowds thronging in. He and Chris took their places unobtrusively off to one corner. Johnny looked up at his mother, his eyes searching out hers. She smiled.

If you are tired of the load of your sins, the choir sang, *let Jesus come into your heart.*

It was another of those songs that always made Johnny restless, unusually restless that night.

The sermon began. An evangelist naturally wants his message to be personal, no matter how many people make up the audience. That night, however, the message seemed to relate particularly to one person's specific needs. Johnny's needs. He grew increasingly restless, thrashing about in his chair. His nervousness intensified as my message concluded and I introduced the evening's invitation.

In those days I used the traditional form, asking people to bow their heads. Then I would invite those who reconized their need to receive Christ to raise their hands.

My eyes drifted toward Johnny and Chris. I saw him try to lift his hand. I knew how disturbed he was. Yet we had made no plans about permitting him to give public witness of his decision—except back in our home church.

Over in their corner of the stadium Johnny grew insistent. Chris tried to quiet him. But then she thought of something. What if, as we drove back home the following day, we had an accident and our son's life was snuffed out?

Click! Click! Click!

Johnny's insistence the previous evening had been light in comparison with now. In my invitation I stressed that this was the final night of our crusade, the last opportunity to be among the many who had committed their lives to Christ. The words incited all the more our son's insistence.

Click! Click! Click!

Chris bent over, bringing her mouth close to Johnny's ear, and whispered, "All right, we'll go down to the front."

He thrust his body forward—so intently that, with just a bit more effort, he might have fallen forward onto the field.

Slowly at first, so imperceptibly that scarcely anyone noticed, Chris pushed Johnny's wheelchair onto the end zone and across the playing field. Except for those sitting in the immediate area, I saw what was happening before the crowd did. I was so startled that everything around me went into a momentary blur. For Chris, as she told me later, it was much more difficult than the night when as a young girl she had made her own commitment to Christ. But she knew just as clearly that it was the right thing to do, the most important event in our son's lifetime.

Any misgivings my wife and I may have had about exhibitionism became needless. This was no stunt with Johnny. He wanted to make a public profession of his faith in Jesus Christ. He wanted to do it that night.

The truth of our son's motivation swept across that stadium audience like an electrical charge. From the impact of Johnny's witness, his unashamed courage, a whole new dimension was introduced to the meeting. Many who otherwise might have put off longer their decision to receive Christ came forward.

By the time she reached the altar area, Chris had sublimated her own embarrassment. She became, instead, another of the personal workers, tenderly guiding a seeker to the foot of the Cross. Johnny was not her son in that moment but rather a truly penitent youth, sorry for his sins, eager to enter into a transforming encounter with the Lord Jesus.

Chris opened her Bible and, along with the others counseling those who had come, carefully explained the plan of salvation.

> *All have sinned and come short of the glory of God.*
> *Christ Jesus came into the world to save sinners.*
> *Christ dies for our sins, was buried, rose again.*
> *Whosoever shall call upon the name of the Lord shall be saved.*

Johnny had heard those verses many times before, good seed from the bins above. Now the words took

Life and thrust their roots into his heart.

"Lord Jesus," Chris prayed quietly, leading Johnny, "I know I am a sinner."

"Yeah," Johnny responded.

"I know Jesus died on the Cross to save me from my sins."

"Yeah."

"And now, right here, I accept Jesus as my own personal Savior."

"Yeah! Yeah!"

It was majestic and beautiful, tearful and exuberant, as our boy became a new person that night. "If any one is in Christ," the Bible tells us, "he is a new creature; old things are passed away; all things become new." It happened to Johnny that night.

No final night of any previous crusade had ever concluded on such a note of triumph. What a family reunion we had back at the room.

"Not only was Johnny's life changed tonight," Chris said, tears flooding her eyes, "but I'll never be the same person again either."

At the height of our sharing, someone knocked on the door. It was the chairman of the committee, blurting, "You can't leave!" His eyes fell upon Johnny. "God bless you, son. You touched us all tonight." Silence hovered over the room for a moment. "Stay another week, Dr. Haggai," the chairman continued. "There's a tremendous moving of the Holy Spirit in this town. You must stay!"

We stayed. And it was one of the most fruitful weeks in my calling as an evangelist—in Johnny's and my callings, I should say, as we shared together in the ministry God had given to us.

THIRTEEN

FOLLOWING the experience on the football field, life took on new dimensions for our son. Gospel hymns that once made him so restless now brought a look of glowing identification to his face. The next time I scheduled a message on eternal lostness, we decided to take Johnny. He listened intently. The old fidgeting was gone.

We saw his confidence and faith blossom more and more through the years—in working with him on Bible memorization, in the obvious involvement he expressed when we prayed with him.

Then, when Johnny was a teen-ager, Chris and Johnny accompanied me on a crusade in San Diego. Frequently on Sunday afternoons during a crusade, I brought a message just for young people—dealing very openly with their problems. We had never permitted Johnny to go. It was, frankly speaking, difficult to know how to deal with sexual matters. Ought we to try to shelter him, at least somewhat, realizing he would never be able to express himself normally toward a wife?

When Johnny heard me announce a Sunday afternoon youth meeting during the crusade in San Diego, he made evident his desire to attend. We decided to let him.

Following the message I gave an invitation directed especially to Christian young people, urging them to let the Holy Spirit have complete possession of their lives: their talents, time, physical drives, everything. Not until Chris and I see him again in heaven will we know what really went through Johnny's mind. He reacted immediately to the invitation. Even before the first young person headed toward the altar, Johnny began the "click! click!" on his wheel chair.

"You're sure?" Chris whispered.

"Yeah!" he replied. His eyes beamed as Chris pushed him forward.

Once again, at the evangelistic service, there was no questioning his sincerity. Or the validity of what happened in his heart.

"You can be just as effective for the Lord as any of those young people," Chris told him afterward. "More than anything else, God needs those who will pray. Your Daddy needs your prayers. You could become a prayer warrior, standing with your Daddy in the great desire he has to reach people."

"Yeah!" Johnny exclaimed.

As Johnny grew older he did emulate the boy Jesus and grow "in wisdom . . . and in favor with God and man." But of course he could not grow "in stature." His physical problems amplified, then multiplied.

As a result, soon after, I said to Chris, "We must get more help for you two, even if we have to hire people to work in shifts."

"It's one thing to hire someone, but another to find a person who would even try to cope with the demands of Johnny's condition," Chris replied.

"At least we can try."

One afternoon when Mother Barker insisted Chris get away for a few hours, she spent them with a dear friend. "I understand there are young women in Northern Ireland anxious to come to America," her friend said. "Some people I know just placed an ad in one of the newspapers and found an excellent girl right away."

So we advertised in the Belfast *Telegraph*. That was how it happened that the mail one day brought a letter from Christina Megrath, a marvelous young woman who played a significant role in Johnny's final years.

Being by nature such a private person, Chris admits to considerable misgivings between the time we sent off a letter of invitation to Lisburn, Northern Ireland, and the day we drove to the airport to meet Christina. Would it be a wise decision to bring someone from so far away? Suppose she didn't fit? What if temperaments clashed? Would she be competent? If Johnny rejected her, what then?

Similar questions had tormented Christina. Victim of an unhappy childhood, intensely introverted, she had been challenged by Gladys Aylward, the famous "Small Woman" of China made internationally famous by the motion picture *The Inn of the Sixth Happiness*.

"I was going to write Miss Aylward," Christina later told my wife. "I was just twenty-one. I wanted my life to glorify my Lord. But then all that childhood trauma got the best of me, and I suffered a nervous breakdown."

It was while Christina was convalescing that her mother saw our ad in the Belfast paper. "Maybe this is what you need," she told her daughter. "You want to do missionary work with children. Wouldn't it be some kind of missionary work taking care of this boy?"

The suggestion in no way appealed to Christina. Not at first. She had never been out of Ireland. Even the thought of missionary service, deep though the burden had been upon her heart, brought specters of terror to the prospect of leaving home and friends for extended periods of time.

Looking after Johnny probably would not be classified by some as missionary work, though our son had a mission. We're convinced that God had prepared Christina to share in that mission. Eventually she became equally convinced. So the God who interlaces the pattern of our lives into a fabric resplendent with his will began speaking to that compassionate and sensitive young woman.

Billy Flannigan, a friend of ours in Belfast, agreed to interview prospective applicants.

"Go ahead and apply," Christina's mother urged.

"It wouldn't do any good," she said. "They would

never give me the job." She resisted for several days. During that time, while we back in America prayed for God's leading, the burden grew heavier upon Christina's heart. "Lord," she prayed, "are you trying to tell me something? Do you really want me to do this work? I want to serve you as a missionary, not a nursemaid." It was one of her besetting sins, she told Chris later, to try to help the Lord decide what he should or shouldn't do with her life.

At last, reluctantly, she wrote to the Belfast address for an interview. A letter promptly came from Billy Flannigan giving her the day when she should come to Belfast, some twenty miles from Lisburn. But she didn't go.

The burden intensified. "I wept myself to sleep at nights," she says. "I tried to tell myself it was only my nervous condition. Yet the conviction grew heavier and heavier. My sense of God's calling to missionary service had never been as heavy as that."

Christina decided to put the Lord to the test, to do as Gideon did and ask for a "fleece." If it was really God's will for her to take the position in America, she wanted to receive a second letter—an unlikely event, she reasoned, since she had failed to show up for the initial interview. To her consternation, two weeks later another letter came.

Her rebellion intensified. The sound of an airplane overhead would terrorize her. How could she possibly make the long trip to the United States? Alone? Meet people she had never known before? Take care of an invalid approaching manhood?

We had sent her a small photograph of Johnny.

She tried not to look at it. She had even wanted to discard it, but instead had placed it in her Bible where it seemed to become a kind of sacred property. As she spent more and more time with her Bible, searching for guidance, she saw more and more of Johnny's picture.

"There was something about that face," she told Chris. "I could see the evidence of much physical suffering, but I also saw Johnny's spiritual qualities. Here I was, an almost hopeless introvert. There was a boy who couldn't talk, couldn't walk, couldn't feed himself. What possible ministry could there be, apart from perhaps making life a little bit easier for his parents?"

There was also the second letter from Billy Flannigan, the fleece she had asked God to send. So, she realized, her rebellion was not primarily a matter of Johnny, or whether or not to go to the United States —but whether she sincerely wanted God's will for her life. She found herself softly singing, "Where He leads me, I will follow." The next day she took the bus into Belfast.

When Billy Flannigan opened the door and looked at her, he said, "I believe you're the person we're looking for!" Christina was speechless.

At the airport the big jet which would thrust her through the skies toward America looked like some monster out of the dark ages.

"I sat half paralyzed the whole trip," she dared to admit months later. "I didn't even hear the stewardess announce we were to fasten our seat belts during takeoff, so she fastened it for me. Through the night we ran into a lot of turbulence. I couldn't think of food. I was too frightened even to go to the lavatory."

She deplaned in Washington and transferred there for a flight to Atlanta. A half hour before scheduled arrival, a torrential storm moved into the area from the west. Intense lightning slashed open the skies. The plane was buffeted back and forth. When the wheels touched down in Atlanta, such fierce lightning ignited the skies that Christina was sure the plane had crashed.

But from the first moment we set eyes on her, the special gift God had sent us from Ireland, our whole family fell in love with her. And she with us. Chris drew her into her arms and kissed her. Johnny's acceptance was visible.

Our own apprehensions were as unfounded as hers. Christina fit our domestic patterns perfectly. She became "family," almost immediately. And coming to America was for her as wondrous as a trip to the moon. She thought of America as a fairyland, although there were inevitable disillusions—and occasional disagreements with Chris and Mother Barker. But Christina adjusted.

Chris soon found she could turn full responsibilities over to her, both physical and spiritual. Christina fixed Johnny's breakfast and took care of him from 8:30 in the morning until 7:30 at night, except for a couple of hours' rest in the afternoon. It was a tremendous respite for my wife, allowing her freedom she hadn't known before. But, most important, Christina Megrath had been sent by God to make a profound contribution to our son's mental and spiritual development. When he had responded to the invitation at the Sunday afternoon youth meeting in San Diego, it was no idle incident. God had a plan for that young man's life, and sent Christina Megrath to help him fit into that plan.

FOURTEEN

OW DOES ONE describe suffering? Johnny's suffering was voluminous, penetrating, saturating his body from head to foot, from ear to ear, from fingertip to fingertip. It spoke to you from his eyes, in the cruel muteness of his lips, the faltering reach of his hand, the inertia that was like chains on his feet.

We recognized his pain. We never escaped its presence. But the joy of knowing Johnny was that he wouldn't let us make pain the prime characteristic of his being. Johnny rose above that pain to become a bundle of curiosity, a fountain of love and concern for others, an unfettered spirit.

I minister far more effectively because of the influence that Johnny had upon me. Johnny was my son biologically, but he was my compatriot in our mutual relationship as children of God.

One visitor said, "I've been in homes where everything was hush-hush about a disadvantaged child. But the way you introduced me to your son made me feel I was meeting a dignitary." Which, so far as I am concerned, he was.

Everything I accomplished and enjoyed, Johnny had the capacity to accomplish and enjoy. He may well have had the ability to surpass me. In fact I'm certain of it. When I traveled, I thought of Johnny. It's been my privilege to meet many outstanding people, and I met them all with the wish that Johnny could meet them too. So Johnny Haggai, in a unique way, was at both the hub and circumference of my ministry.

From his earliest days of childhood, when the sound of my voice evoked such an immediate response from him, we grew closer and closer in spirit. It was a beautifully robust experience, though we never had a normal child-father relationship. We were much more man-to-man.

I made it a point to keep in close touch by telephone. Chris often placed the phone by Johnny's ear and, sometimes for as much as half an hour, I chatted with him on the same level I would speak with anyone.

Johnny's conversion "took." He became more considerate, less demanding, more tolerant. He was "a new creation in Christ Jesus," as one translation of the Bible depicts the "born again" experience. But of much greater significance, his devotion to functions of the spirit multiplied. He wanted to commit more and more portions of Scripture to memory, to invest more and more hours—and I do mean hours—in prayer. His intercessions devoted less time to aunts and uncles and aches and pains and increasingly more time to people's spiritual destiny and the eternal dimensions of their lives.

Given his disability and necessarily cloistered lifestyle, Johnny could have developed a monastic mentality. Actually, the outer shell of our son was a ruse, a camouflage. Inside lived a puckish spirit, a bounding adventurer, a quarterback, a left-fielder.

It is, of course, important for a father and son to be physical with each other. From early childhood I tussled with Johnny often, and he loved it. When he grew older, he loved to arm wrestle. He had considerable strength. He could grab you and almost bring the blood to your hand. He was a fierce competitor who detested losing. He wanted to participate in sports, bowling, badminton. We let him try whatever he could. Chess fascinated him. We tried to teach him, and he caught on, but the game is so slow. By the time we asked him for a decision on all the options of a move, it became too frustrating for him.

It frustrated him terribly to be so dependent upon other people from the time he got up until the time he went to bed, so Chris and I tried to alleviate that as much as we could. But he was impetuous. He made up his mind quickly and liked immediate action.

Because he had so much pain and discomfort, he invariably became restless when taken into public places, particularly church. He was so prejudiced toward my preaching—my number one adherent—

that he didn't concentrate when someone else occupied the pulpit.

The first time we took him to a crusade was in Mobile, Alabama. He had never seen such a crowd of people. Pride rose like a sunburst in his eyes, to think that big crowd had come just to hear his father preach. It excited him to such outcries that Chris had to scold him. He tried to be quiet but again and again he forgot himself, becoming increasingly noisy. Chris could see it bothered people, so she took him out—whereupon he burst into sobbing.

"Johnny," Chris told him, "I'm not punishing you. It's just that we've got to be quiet when Daddy preaches. Otherwise people who don't know the Lord Jesus will be disturbed and won't hear the message he has for them."

"Is this Dr. Haggai's son?" people began to ask, coming up to Chris and Johnny at crusade meetings.

"Yeah!" Johnny would sing out.

The time came when he wanted to be up on the platform with me. I would gladly have permitted it because it would have meant so much to Johnny, but we knew some people would accuse us of exploiting him.

If you really wanted to get on Johnny's good side, you needed only to speak of how much he and I resembled each other. And he always wanted to be identified with my ethnic background, Syria—and, more distinctly, the Arab race.

"Are you an American?" we sometimes asked him.

"Umn!" would be his curt response.

"Are you Syrian?"

"Yeah!"

He loved his country but also revelled in his foreign roots. With the passing of time he developed deep concern for the spiritual needs of Arabs. It hurt him to hear negative reports from the Muslim world, of so few ever hearing the gospel, much less turning to the Lord. I doubt that I should say Johnny became anti-Israel; certainly Chris and I are not. He did realize, however, as do we, that many Christians emphasize Israel at the expense of neglecting Arabs. You perhaps know that the majority of Christians in the nation of Israel are non-Hebrew, and mostly Arabs. Surveys indicate substantially less than 500 Christian Jews in the country—magnificent Christians, I should add, many of them suffering intense and sustained persecution because of their faith and witness.

My father, who is Syrian from ear to ear and head to foot, enjoyed special rapport with his grandson. Johnny would listen ten times in a day to accounts of his grandfather's background.

My father nearly lost his life as a young man. The Turks were in control of Syria. They drafted Syrian boys into the army at the age of twenty. Christians could be virtually certain they would not come back alive because they were always pushed into the most dangerous positions.

My father and his two older brothers, determined to flee to America, headed out by horse-drawn carriage from Damascus toward Beirut. A soldier stopped them and asked where they were going. Only for a joy ride, they told him. He looked underneath the carriage, however, saw they had provisions for a long trip, and arrested them.

My father was the youngest, and the soldiers

thought he would be the easiest to crack. But he stuck to that story and insisted he and his brothers were only going on a joy ride.

"You tell us the truth," the soldiers threatened, "or we'll have you beheaded."

Suddenly a man appeared with authentic credentials from the Sultan of Turkey. "How dare you do this to friends of the Sultan?" he asked.

Immediately the three brothers were released.

To this day my father has no idea who the deliverer was.

Johnny also liked to hear a subsequent anecdote about the time my father walked down a street one Sunday morning shortly after his arrival in this country and heard worshipers singing "Onward Christian Soldiers." He instinctively cringed, afraid they might be oppressors preparing to move out onto the streets.

His grandfather's experiences as a youth helped Johnny relate more clearly to the deprivation suffered by people throughout the Third World. It helped him see the Arabs as oppressed people.

Because Johnny became so interested in all aspects of my ministry, he not only visited my office but Chris arranged for him to attend occasional staff meetings. Sitting for any length of time was always a problem for him. But he would sit for long hours at staff meetings, his only sound being agreement or disagreement with some subjects. He responded spontaneously at times but usually only if we asked for his opinion.

We tried to watch him carefully, because there was invariably a price to pay. He became so emotionally involved at staff meetings, so physically weary from hours inert in his chair, that afterward he sometimes had such fits of vomiting we feared for his life. But whatever the price, Johnny never turned down an opportunity to sit in on sessions.

It is no exaggeration to say that our son knew the inner workings of Haggai Institute just as intimately as any staff or board member; for, though his participation had to be limited, we kept him well informed. A common occurrence, the moment I entered the house, was to go to Johnny's room for a briefing.

I usually lifted both of his hands, a mode of contact he liked. "We had a really rough one today," I might say. "I'm bushed." I could see empathy rise on his face. "I don't know how we're going to handle all these programs, Johnny. We're as careful as we know how to be with finances, but there's never enough money to do what we've got to do. Yet we must move ahead. We can't fall back."

"Yeah!" Johnny would agree.

"You know, ol' Buddy, it never ceases to amaze me what it takes to get people to support good causes. Show pictures of starving children, people blown to bits by war or made homeless by a flood or an earthquake, and money comes in. But talk to people about evangelism in the Third World—you know, helping people to reach their own people no westerner can reach, and . . ."

Softly Johnny would respond, "Yeah."

I couldn't properly share Johnny's story without telling you something about his unique career as a prayer warrior. For that's what he became, Lieutenant Johnny Haggai, you might say, up front with the troops, giving battle to the forces of evil.

One thing is absolutely sure. I've never met anyone who became more enthusiastic about this ministry to the Third World. Perhaps I should have shared even more of the problems with him. I'm not sure. But I did keep him fully informed about challenges and victories. That became therapy for me, emphasizing the positives, and, most important, knowing Johnny was praying and praising God for the victories and trusting him for the challenges. The older he became, the stronger grew Johnny's confidence in God.

"I'm going to need ten thousand dollars by Monday noon," I might tell him.

You could be sure Johnny would awaken bright and early come Monday, waiting for me to call. He knew the call would convey positive information—because, uniquely, Johnny was in partnership with me. We were, as the Bible says, "laborers together with God."

FIFTEEN

THE MINISTRY of evangelism challenged me increasingly. I value the individual. I believe that personal evangelism is the most effective. But I also enjoyed seeing God's work progress quantitatively. The attendances grew larger. Some of the ministers and laymen in our circle of friends were constantly predicting substantial growth in the years just ahead. Several Christian leaders, convinced that the ministry was destined to achieve larger and larger influence, contacted me about a full-time relationship in a supportive role. But the Lord had other plans—plans for which Johnny had been brought into this world and endowed with the gifts necessary for a lifetime of distinguished service.

Johnny visited the office frequently and attended

more and more of the crusades. Despite his problems, I looked forward to his attendance at a crusade as much as he anticipated being there. He couldn't have generated more enthusiasm if I had been coach of the Dallas Cowboys taking them into the Super Bowl. Though Chris counseled with him and urged him to control himself, he became more vocally involved in the services than before. He developed his own articulation of "amen" and would call out in disturbing acclamation at some part of the sermon that particularly met his approval.

It would have been a father's justifiable prerogative simply to tell Johnny he couldn't attend anymore. But I wanted him involved, especially as I became aware of how earnestly he prayed for every detail of the ministry.

At each crusade, at one of the initial sessions I introduced Johnny from the pulpit. I told people he was as normal as any young person in the audience, only handicapped. I did my utmost to speak of his handicap in such a manner that would dispel thoughts of our wanting sympathy.

Johnny reveled in those introductions. Of course, as he grew older he became much more aware of the differences between himself and other youth. Yet one of the first steps toward maturity in life consists of accepting ourselves. For the Christian such acceptance has an added dimension: accepting ourselves in the will of God. Psychologists tell us that one of our problems as human beings can be outright self-hatred. I feel sorry for people I meet, especially Christians, who show inclinations toward self-rejection. They may be physically unattractive. They may feel intellectually inferior. They see themselves as low in the social ladder. Well, the God who chose a different blueprint for every snowflake certainly has a purpose for every human being he designs. I like to think of Johnny as one of God's special snowflakes.

Few parents realize how important it is to the development of their children's character and personality for the parent to accept the children for what they are and to make that positive sense of acceptance both natural and obvious. That rules out the doting mother and bragging father who push their children like booking agents—not so much for the child's good as for the inflation of their own parental image.

Some people might accuse me of being glib about Johnny or say I'm only trying to veneer the painful facts about him. But not so. People assess misfortune in direct ratio to their world and life view. A materialist would see Johnny as a tragic genetic mistake. But God helped Chris and me to see—with clarity and in awe—that Johnny illustrates how unimportant the physical side of life becomes when we measure it beside what is eternal within us.

People sensed our acceptance of Johnny. Even yet I marvel as I think of how absolutely genuine Chris's attitude toward him was when the two of them appeared in public. That in itself was sufficient to relax people, to encourage them to come to Johnny. And night after night when he attended crusades, people did come to talk to him. Some did it condescendingly; they didn't understand, and didn't know what else to do. But many talked to Johnny as though he were as normal as any of their friends. Johnny relished that.

Such encounters did become counterproductive to a certain extent, in that Johnny felt increasingly at ease in expressing himself. Chris told me he seemed to preach harder than I did, getting so excited on occasion that he nearly took over the service. And when the summer nights were warm, he perspired every bit as much as did those of us on the platform.

After we were able to obtain more help for Chris, she was able to take part in crusade programs and Johnny became her number-one fan. At times he got so excited, from either her singing or my preaching, that he became ill and had to be removed from the audience. Once, at one of the large stadium crusades, he became unusually noisy—outburst after outburst turning people's eyes away from the pulpit and toward Chris and Johnny—that I lost complete continuity a couple of times in my message.

Chris tried to quiet him. But Johnny felt exceptionally good that night and repeatedly forgot himself, which led to one of the rare times I reprimanded him. "You must not make that much noise," I said on the way back to the hotel. "You disturb people." Johnny puckered and then began to cry as though his heart would break. I felt like a dog!

"He loves you so," Chris said. "You know that. We'll try to help him be more cooperative."

As the evangelistic ministry developed, I spent many hours in prayer and introspection. I thank God for the many fruitful evangelistic ministries across North America and wish there were more.

I like to organize projects. God has surrounded me with highly competent people, and I'm confident it would have been possible substantially to enlarge the impact of our evangelistic ministry. Yet the imbalance of witness in the West as contrasted with that in the Third World bothered me increasingly. But beyond those realities, just as back in the pastorate, I sensed a new and strong compulsion.

My visit to West Asia in 1964 convinced me that new methods must be discovered and employed if the gospel of Christ was to reach the peoples of the Third World which is, primarily, the non-Christian world. It was obvious to me that trained national Christian leaders were the ones to penetrate their own areas with the gospel. The West was losing acceptability because of the growing nationalism in the Third World nations and because of the increasing resentment against paternalism, whether real or imaginary.

I had no intention originally of getting into this ministry myself. Three factors, however, intensified my motivation for Third World evangelization. The first was that I found no church group or organization providing the training I felt necessary to meet the need of the Third World. Second, during 1965 and 1966 spiritually perceptive people (both missionaries from the West and leaders from the East) expressed concern over the subtle shift in world mood and the concomitant requirement to change mission strategy. The third factor was the Congress on Evangelism in Berlin which, to me, pointed up the wasteful duplication and overlap in many areas and the shocking gaps in other areas.

In 1968, at the behest of Indonesian leaders, I led an evangelistic effort in Jakarta, Indonesia. But, effective as this effort was (the first time in Indonesian history when Pentecostals and Presbyterians, the two largest groups in that country, cooperated along with the other denominational groups), the largest impact of all was the influence of the Indonesian people on me. I met many leaders who asked questions about my methods as an evangelist. Perceptive questions. As a result I conducted a brief seminar for them on the "how" of evangelism, and that seminar reinforced the idea born during my 1964 West Asia visit.

At first, because I wasn't sure, I sheltered the idea in secrecy. I like to weigh new potentials carefully, sifting them, exploring them. But "nothing can withstand the force of an idea whose time has come." Thus the following year, in the autumn, we announced a seminar in Switzerland, inviting credentialed leaders from several Third World nations.

Of that seminar, men like Roland J. Payne from Liberia, holder of two academic doctorates, said, "I will never forget the ministry and witness we encountered in Switzerland. What you started here should have been started twenty years ago."

I was both elated and perturbed. Enthusiasm for missionary endeavor has long been on the wane in North America. Christian publishers, for example, shy away from books with overseas settings or themes. Americans at times have a frighteningly narrow view of the world and the church's mission.

"You know," I told Johnny, "that could be both good and bad, maybe more good than bad. Missionaries have done a great job across the world but they've had to learn by mistakes as well as by success. One of the mistakes, a very big mistake, has been the effort by missionaries to bring Asians, for example, to a Western understanding of Christianity rather than presenting the gospel in an Asian context."

I thank God for the traditional Western missionary, because I am a second-generation product. Presbyterian missionaries took the gospel to Damascus, Syria, in the last century, and at the turn of the century my father's uncle came to know Christ as his personal Savior and Lord. He, in turn, won my father to faith in Christ.

Discussions like that electrified Johnny. One of my first anticipations of heaven is to discover just how succinctly he comprehended such concepts. It was Johnny's reaction to potential ministry in the Third World, as much as anything else, that helped me see a clear pattern of divine guidance.

Building on the initial Switzerland seminar pattern, we began further exploration into the Third World. Dr. Ernest Watson, a man of distinctive leadership capabilities, joined our staff as dean. Humanly speaking, Haggai Institute could never have survived without "dear Dr. Watson." And so began the laborious task of winning people's confidence abroad and encouraging stewardship and prayer partnership at home.

I continued holding evangelistic meetings and crusades in the Third World. "But, you know," I told Johnny, "much as I enjoy those crusades, I don't feel right about them. It's past time for such people to take full responsibility for evangelism in their own cultures."

The new ministry required extensive travel overseas. From the outset I sent tapes back for Johnny. I recorded interviews, dictated summaries and impressions, introduced Johnny to a multitude of new friends. Consequently, men like General John Huwae of Indonesia, one of our earliest Haggai Institute alumni, became special people to our son. So did George Samuel, United Nations consultant in nuclear medicine, as well as many others.

Home again from our second seminar in Switzerland, I gave Johnny a complete briefing. "It's nice having the seminar in Switzerland," I said. "I guess that's about the most beautiful place on the face of the earth. But it really bothers me. Those men are leaders. They know how to think. But I still believe it would be better if we could conduct our institutes in the Third World itself. There are too many examples of nationals trained in the West who become spoiled by the West and cannot effectively relate to their own people."

Johnny agreed.

So in 1971 what is now Haggai Institute moved to Singapore. There were compelling reasons for that move.

In the first place, the climate and cuisine in Switzerland are not compatible to the life style of most of the people of the Third World. They are accustomed to rice every day in their menus and to a more tropical temperature in their environment.

Then there was the language problem. All of the leaders coming for training are proficient in English, but few of them are proficient in German. Therefore, if any of them missed a plane connection and came in late, they could not communicate. They did not know how to contact us, and we did not know when they arrived.

The days of 1969 and 1970 were also days of the

hijacking craze. Much hijacking was taking place over that part of the world. Since almost all the flights coming from the South Pacific, the Orient, and the Subcontinent stopped either in Tel Aviv, Beirut, or Cairo, there was a psychological problem. To put it frankly, the men were just plain, downright scared, and no thinking person could blame them for that. By meeting in Singapore, we eliminated this problem.

One of the major reasons for moving was that while Switzerland is a neutral nation, it is also a nation associated with affluence. When the average American, for instance, thinks of Switzerland, he does not think of sacrificial giving to world evangelization. Rather, he thinks of numbered bank accounts, ski holidays, and luxurious vacations.

There was yet one more reason for the move. It took two and a half hours to transport the participants from the airport (Zurich) to the venue, which was near Interlaken. In Singapore, they can be any place on the island within thirty minutes' time.

It has long since been the consensus of the leaders of the organization that Singapore is the ideal location. The subsequent years since the move have borne this out.

The program accelerated to two five-week sessions annually, then four, plus many shorter institutes in other areas—and then increasingly wider outreach. Most important of all are training programs launched by the leaders themselves as they transmit to their fellow Christian leaders what they have learned in Singapore.

I think, for example, of Abraham DeLove in Ghana.

He came to Singapore, having just led the Head of State of his country to Christ. He returned to Ghana with a reservoir of information and enthusiasm—joining other alumni in his country, with his president's special blessing and cooperation, in an effort to make Ghana a model of Christian nationhood in troubled Africa. During late June and early July of 1977, the Head of State and Chairman of the Supreme Military Council, General Kutu Acheampong proclaimed a week of repentance and meditation. The Reverend Mr. DeLove was asked to officiate at this and preach the major sermon.

There were men like Jose Nebab of the Philippines, who left Singapore ablaze and has kept the fire burning ever since.

We have had disappointments, as does any educational institution. Our critics tend to emphasize our occasional failures and ignore the successes.

The faculty includes such men as Dr. Chandu Ray, formerly the renowned Anglican bishop of Pakistan; Dr. Kyung Chick Han of Korea, pastor-emeritus of the world's largest Presbyterian Church.; Dr. Lee Won Sul, newspaper columnist, secretary-general of the International Association of University Presidents, and dean of the graduate school of Seoul, Korea's Kyung Hee University; George Samuel, previously mentioned; Dr. Timothy Yu, head of the communications department of Hong Kong University; and others of this caliber.

We use Third World experts to train and challenge Third World leaders. The training becomes much more relevant to those who attend, and much more acceptable to their fellow nationals back home. The key is *leadership*. One of the past problems in foreign missions has been a timidity and/or an inability to go after the leaders.

The whole world began to come alive to Johnny. He wanted to see all the news on television, lest he miss something about the Third World. Heads of state in the Third World became like special friends because they were among the leaders with whom we had personal and meaningful communication.

Although Johnny never owned a billfold and had never spent a dollar on his own, he had a keen sense of the value and utilization of money. One of our board members came back from a visit to the Third World in 1973 and suggested that nationals fund their own programs instead of looking to Haggai Institute for economic sustenance. Johnny exclaimed with delighted approval. You would have thought he had been elected treasurer of the corporation and knew firsthand the burden of carrying our program.

I mentioned American Christians losing their vision for world evangelization. I wish such Christians could have met Johnny. He clearly understood the Savior's mandate: "into all the world." He understood how impoverished a Christian's life can become if he or she doesn't have a vision and compassion for all those the Savior included when he hung on the Cross and walked away from his tomb.

Only one aspect of my shift in emphasis to overseas bothered Johnny, the three-week separations. During the years of my U.S. ministry, I was usually home every other week. When I was gone more than that, he and Chris could join me. So we had to be careful how we discussed overseas plans. For, in spite of his concern for the Third World, Johnny never quite overcame the emotional trauma of having his father gone away from home, especially out of the country.

With Johnny becoming more and more identified with the ministry, we tried to think of better ways in which he could express his interest. One of our staff members suggested having a few of the report letters go out over Johnny's signature. I liked the idea. So did Chris. It would have been a whole new horizon for Johnny, to have drafted the letter with his cooperation and then show him the completed project. But we just couldn't bring ourselves to it. Wonderful as people were to our son, sympathetic and understanding in so many ways, we simply could not do anything to give the impression of using him to prey upon people's sympathy.

"There are many things you won't be able to do," Chris told Johnny. "But what you can do is give your life to the most important work for God here on earth. You can give your life to prayer: prayer for your father and for Christian workers everywhere."

She will always remember the look in his eyes, the affirmation and resolution, as he answered softly, "Yeah."

Johnny remained his normal self. A disciple of joy. Inquisitive about the immediate world around him. Full of fun. Yet he launched upon a career of intercession just as surely and as avidly as he would have entered some other career had he been endowed with the physical facility to do so. Chris helped him develop a prayer list, an extensive one. She wrote down names—but to help us remember, not Johnny. Once he added a person or project to his list, he never forgot. Christina became especially adept at helping Johnny with his prayer time. A deeply devout person herself, she would gladly have served exclusively as intercessory assistant. But I reserved many sessions for just myself and our son. I never got so close to him in any other way.

Of course, Chris had even more opportunities than I. Our procedure was to voice a name or a need and then give Johnny time to lift the person or project silently to the attention of his Lord. We dared not forget an item on the list. If we did, Johnny always protested. It wasn't enough simply to insert the name or circumstance then and there. No, he wanted to go all the way back to the beginning of the list and pray for each project once more, this time properly including everyone and everything.

You may ask why we needed to help him at all, why he couldn't program names and needs into his memory bank and then proceed on his own. Well, first of all, Johnny was intensely gregarious. He loved his family. But I believe he especially wanted to be with those close to him during times of prayer. And there may have been another factor. Unable to articulate for himself, but alert to every spoken word, perhaps he loved the sound of words more than we knew and wanted the sacred time of prayer to include audible sound as well as silent voicings. I wonder how broad a vocabulary he did have. I wonder if he enjoyed words the way I do. Maybe Johnny was extremely eloquent in the deep silences of his peculiar existence.

He wanted to remember all the delegates attending a session in Singapore, all the faculty. But if we mentioned a special need for one of the participants or faculty members—as, for example, when George Samuel had a special need regarding the health of one of his children—Johnny would halt procedures immediately upon the mention of the person's name. "We forget someone, Buddy?" I asked, the time George had that special need.

"Yeah."

"Is it something about George Samuel himself?"

"Yeah."

"Did I tell you about some special assignment he has this month for the U.N.?"

"Umn."

"He has some personal need?"

"Umn! Umn! Umn!"

"Oh, I get it. His new baby—"

"Yeah!"

I've rarely been able to pray for hours on a given subject. I state the situation to God, as clearly and briefly as possible, and that's it. Not so with Johnny. He didn't limit his prayer life to times when one of us prayed with him. We might find him, quiet in his chair, his head resting to the side. Because of his continual health needs, it was necessary to keep close surveillance at all times.

"Sleepy?" one of us might ask.

"Umn."

Then we understood, and stepped quietly back, surmising that our son was in private audience with the One who said, "Call unto me, and I will answer you, and show you great and mighty things. . . . the effectual, fervent prayer of a righteous man availeth much."

SIXTEEN

TO TELL Johnny's story completely, I need to share with you something deeply intimate and immeasurably beautiful. Christina Megrath. That amazing young woman came to us so shy she all but trembled at the sound of her name. When we had visitors, even people who came often, she immediately disappeared. It took many months before she gave the slightest evidence of beginning to overcome her shyness. But she and Johnny very quickly established vital and vibrant rapport.

Christina came to us in her early thirties, with Johnny in his late teens. I must say very frankly that the two feel deeply in love with each other. But let me carefully explain. Our world today—so emotionally sick, so starved for even basic values—knows frighteningly little of the kind of attachment the two acquired for each other. I've told you how normal Johnny was, of his awareness of attractive girls. One of the most frustrating aspects of his physical prison surely involved his complete inability to relate to those of the opposite sex in any normal way.

Beautifully, Christina met Johnny's need for a profoundly meaningful relationship. But how can I describe it? It was more than male and female, far more. It was more than brother and sister, though that perhaps comes close to a definition. Christina was far too moral a person for any kind of cheap relationship, too intelligent to presume anything romantic. Perhaps platonic is the word to use. Or idyllic. Or better still, I should say that our Creator, who never lacks capacity to innovate, created for our son and Christina a relationship unique in human emotion.

My communication with Christina was limited mostly to pleasantries. And I had become defensive toward anyone entrusted with our son's care. "How is the Irish girl doing?" I would ask.

Chris assured and reassured me. One day Chris said, "I think the best way to evaluate is to say that Christina shows Johnny absolutely no pity whatever." Then I really became defensive! Chris smiled, touched my hand, and said, "She treats him as a normal person. I was talking to her yesterday and she told me—you could see how completely sincere she was—that she simply does not see abnormality in Johnny. She sees *Johnny* instead. She has a deep and beautiful love for him. She respects him and accepts him as a person."

The more Chris and I think in retrospect about

Christina, and the more I think about the attitude Chris had toward our son, the more convinced I am that God gave to all of us a special insight. It was a gift, a divine gift. Without that gift, we not only would have failed to enrich Johnny's life but, in so failing, we would have impoverished ourselves.

As I've indicated, the natural inclination of many people on meeting Johnny was to condescend. I'm sure it amused Johnny many times to have people talk down to him, even though it distracted him. "He's so dear," someone said once when we had Johnny in public. "Does he understand what's going on around him?"

"He's as sharp as either of us!" I snapped to one such observer. "Verbal competence doesn't necessarily indicate intelligence, you know!"

Or some dowager would sing out, "Isn't he the sweetest little man?" adding, "Wasn't your Mamma nice to get you all cleaned up and dressed and let you come to hear your Daddy preach?"

Imagine talking to a normal adolescent in that manner. It happened to Johnny over and over—because of his overwhelming handicap, to be sure, but also because of the equally overwhelming handicap in the minds of adults who ought to have known better.

When Johnny passed through his adolescent years, he was a fully normal adolescent in disguise. A fully normal teenager. Thank God, Chris and I saw that. And so did Christina.

Condescension occurs not only in the things we say but in the way we say things. Tone of voice. Facial mannerisms. And perhaps more than all of these, unwillingness or inability to be candid.

Christina, introverted though she was among others, could be wonderfully candid with our son. Her deep Irsih accent and rich Ulster idioms fascinated Johnny. "Have just a wee taste," she would say, if some particular food didn't catch his fancy. "Come on now, have a go at it."

There were times at first when Mother Barker and my wife couldn't quite understand Christina. But Johnny understood.

"Sure you do!" Christina sang out one day. "If you was to start talkin', it would be in an Irish brogue, now wouldn't it, Johnny? You'd give out the palaver as regular as if you was born in Belfast!"

Johnny howled with delight.

She would humor him with wild, farfetched stories. Old Ireland abounded in tales of leprechauns and cloven hoofs. She related many of Ulster's superstitions to him, the wilder the better. When she heard a new joke, her first impulse was to share it with him, as a delightful camaraderie grew between them.

Johnny enjoyed clothes. At first Chris and Mother Barker bought things and brought them home to him. As he grew older, however, he preferred to shop for himself. Christina could detect as quickly as Chris what would please him and what wouldn't—which gave her opportunities for more teasing. She rarely permitted such opportunities to slip by.

One day, for example, a clerk showed them some styles. He glanced condescendingly at Johnny, seemingly somewhat irritated by the two women's insistence on finding things that pleased him. One suggestion he made was so dull and colorless that Chris wondered why anyone had ever fashioned such cloth in the first place.

"Say, Johnny," Christina said (pretending to be serious), "there's just the duggin's for you! Wear that and people won't be noticing your handsome face all the time."

Johnny rocked back and forth in his wheelchair, overcome with mirth.

"Well," Christina chided impishly, "if I'm to be nothin' but a daisy picker here, then you can choose your own."

Johnny laughed all the harder. And the clerk discovered—as did many people who had similar glimpses of him—that Johnny was a real human being who ought to be treated as such.

Johnny liked to feel fabrics, not just look at them. He shopped for price too and watched for sales like any astute shopper. He understood color matching. When we bought something new, a new shirt for instance, he wanted to wear it right away. (A sure way to make points with him was to compliment something he was wearing.) But even though his mother and her associates gradually learned little things to do to make it less tiring, shopping taxed Johnny's strength. Sometimes he came home too exhausted to give further thought to what had been purchased.

Christina was a comfort on such occasions. In her quiet way, she structured a gentle denouement to the exciting experience, talking to him about the time at the store and the good selection they had made and how pleased everyone would be to see him attired in his new clothes. Quietly, warmly, calming his taut nerves. "Now it's time to rest a skite," she might say. "I'm a wee bit tired myself." So he would rest, slowly unwinding from the exciting experience.

Mother Barker and Chris both wondered at first how Christina would do with the supreme test of feeding Johnny. Mealtime for him could so often be like dressing a sore wound. He tested her at first. Much as he accepted Christina, he had learned to depend upon Chris or her mother at mealtime.

When Christina brought the first morsel to his mouth, he clamped his teeth onto the spoon and looked at her in exploratory defiance. But Christina conducted herself as though it had happened many times. "I know it isn't easy," she said softly, a strain of plaintive music in the tone of her voice. "But you must eat your food. Here, let's see how quickly we can get it all down." Within days his eyes began to brighten when he saw her come with the food, and she soon could feed him faster than anyone.

Infinite patience. That was Christina. But such a contrast to her natural self, so tense and nervous. It was a gift God gave her so she could reach out to Johnny and learn back from him. The routine of his day became the constant newness of total life to her.

We always wanted him to sleep as late in the morning as possible. It could be as late as nine when she slipped into his room, greeted him, gave him a big hug and kiss. Then she got him ready and put on the cloth girdle that gave his body support.

"My, it's a beautiful day, Johnny," she might say, "and I declare it's even prettier seeing the likes of that shining face of yours!"

He relished compliments but always protested any hint of a description of himself that wasn't thoroughly masculine. Christina knew just how to accommodate that trait. For example, Johnny accepted the fact of being unable to control his body functions. He wanted to be clean and he deplored the stench of soiled clothing. He had learned not to be shy when women close to him took care of his body. Yet he also had a keen sense of propriety. While she looked after his intimate needs, Christina had a way of speaking nonchalantly about other things as though they sat in the living room under formal conditions.

Johnny's all-time favorite breakfast was Cream of Wheat. He never tired of it. But he often protested even favorite foods because of the constant difficulty of consuming them. He could only swallow, not chew. So if food were a bit too hot, he couldn't mix saliva with it to temper it.

"When we get to heaven," Christina teased him, "I'll let you feed me. And such a fuss I'm going to make: 'It's too hot. It's not hot enough. Too sweet. Too salty. I'm too chuffy.' See if I don't carry on so loud Gabriel himself will come running to see whatever is the matter. Ah, but it's no mind, Johnny. We're friends, how an' ever the way you take your food."

After breakfast, she took him to the bathroom. A bath, shave, careful attention to grooming his hair.

They devoted much of the morning bath each day to Bible memorization. He cherished Romans 10:9. "If thou shalt confess with thy mouth the Lord Jesus, and shalt believe in thine heart that God hath raised him from the dead, thou shalt be saved." Since he learned verses by having us repeat them for him, phrase by phrase, you could say "If thou shalt confess," pause a moment, and see his anticipation and clear recognition of "with thy mouth the Lord Jesus" register with twinkling excitement in his wide eyes.

Like so many of us, he learned John 3:16 in his earliest childhood. Christina would playfully jumble up the verse sometimes. "For God so loved only Christina Megrath, not the other people of the world," and Johnny would interrupt her, calling out loudly, "Umn! Umn!" until she quoted it correctly. Then he smiled his approval. But he liked for her to mix up a verse. It seemed a vital part of the learning process, even though he appeared distraught when she did it.

She told him Bible stories by the hour. He most enjoyed the story of Joseph and the coat of many colors. His favorite subject was heaven. To hear of the golden streets, the endless day with no need of the sun, the abolition of pain and tears and death, all brought radiant anticipation to his countenance.

Christina read many books to him. He heard the "Sugar Creek Gang" stories many times. He looked forward to each Sunday's edition of *Power,* sent so thoughtfully and faithfully by my mother.

They watched television together, Andy Griffith being one of his favorites. He didn't care for comics, except for *Peanuts.* Lucy was his favorite, her frustrations with Linus and the Beethoven concerts of particular delight.

During the morning bath hour Christina often sang to him. By her own admission she was no singer —so much so she often got out of tune, a situation Johnny promptly made known by bursting into laughter. He urged her to sing, daily.

"I'm not at myself this morning," Christina would

say, if she didn't feel up to song.

Whereupon Johnny became the more insistent.

"I'm onto you, Johnny," Christina might then add. "You want to get me all out of tune so you can have a laugh at me just."

To which Johnny would drawl, "Yeah!"

With that, however out-of-sorts she may have felt, Christina inevitably complied.

Could our son have had perfect pitch, a golden ear? He could have inherited his mother's exceptional talent. We have a lot of questions to be answered, a multitude of anticipations, when we one day see Johnny in his fullness.

I've used a number of different soloists in my ministry. Johnny admired them all and would listen enrapt to every rendition. Perhaps as they sang he too was singing deep down in his heart. He paid special attention to song lyrics, as illustrated by what happened one morning during his bath. Christina had been singing for several minutes. She would begin one hymn, sing as many of the stanzas as she remembered, and then move on to another. In that natural progression she began the first stanza of Frederick Whitfield's magnificent hymn:

> *There is a name I love to hear,*
> *I love to sing its worth.*
> *It sounds like music to my ear,*
> *The sweetest name on earth.*

The song caught our son's fancy, and he became very intent until Christina began the chorus:

> *O how I love Jesus,*
> *O how I love Jesus,*

O how I love Jesus,
Because He first loved me!

Johnny became restless. Thinking he perhaps wanted her to repeat the chorus, Christina sang it again. Johnny became increasingly upset, so, not understanding, she changed to another song. Johnny relaxed, contented again.

Several mornings passed with no singing. Then one day, as morning sunlight streamed into Johnny's window, she again sang "O how I love Jesus," and, again, Johnny grew upset. Christina quickly changed to another song, but it started her thinking. She had such insight when it came to Johnny that she sought to fathom his every whim and response, the better to know him, the better to help him.

One subsequent morning, selecting another stanza, she sang:

It tells me of a Savior's love,
Who died to set me free
It tells me of His precious blood,
The sinner's perfect plea.

Johnny grew apprehensive, his eyes intent upon her as, with all the tenderness she could summon, she began the chorus:

O how I love Jesus!

"Umn! Umn!" Johnny protested.

Christina fell quickly silent, studied him for a moment, and then asked, "What puts you so thrawn, Johnny? Why don't you like me to sing that?"

"Umn! Umn!" he repeated.

She thought a moment, whispered a prayer for wisdom, for understanding, "Is it because you don't want me to love Jesus better than you?" she asked. Now he smiled, big and full and warm. So Christina altered the lyrics to:

O how we love Jesus!

It was like watching a flower bud and bloom, the way Johnny brought Christina out of her shell. Like King Arthur's Merlin, he could draw out of her life rare fragrance and lilting melody.

At first Chris didn't notice the widening contrast between Christina's freeness with Johnny and her stiffness with the rest of us.

"She's like two people," Mother Barker said one day.

So it was. Christina would be working with Johnny, talking to him or reading to him, and then one of us would enter the room. At first she fell immediately silent. Later, as she felt a bit more free with us, she would modify her spirit.

Chris began tactful analysis. Just as with her love and gentleness Christina won her way into our son's heart, so Chris determined to do the same for her.

Christina tended to dress rather drably when she first arrived but, because Johnny liked bright clothes, she responded by selecting colorful attire for herself.

"You look so pretty today," Chris often told her when she appeared in the morning wearing something bright.

She greeted such compliments with skepticism at

first. But Christina is an extremely intelligent person, shy and sensitive partly because of that intelligence. Little by little, she warmed toward my wife and began to open up.

Chris learned little things about her. One time the two of them went shopping together and Christina selected a bright frock Johnny would like. There was a jewelry counter nearby. My wife selected a string of beads. "Wouldn't these add a nice touch?" she asked.

Christina frowned and grew tense. "I'd like to buy them for you if I may," Chris told her. She quickly saw that Christina's reaction had not been prompted by frugality. It occurred to Chris that she had never seen her wearing jewelry. Chris nonchalantly held the jewelry up against the dress, commenting, "See how well they go together."

"But Christian women in my hometown back in Northern Ireland would never wear any such thing," she said.

"What about bright dresses like this one you just purchased?" Chris asked.

Christina blushed.

Thus began the first of many long discussions the two of them had about clothing, makeup, jewelry. "It's not powder or jewelry that makes your relationship to Christ," my wife told her, "It's your heart relationship."

Christina told how, as a child, she occasionally gave vent to her sense of humor, her love for fun. "I would be scolded," she said, "or shunned and ignored just. One day a girl in our meeting place heard about my desire to become a missionary. 'What a lot of palaver,' she said. 'You're too lighthearted to be a Christian,' she said, 'let alone a missionary. It's not for the likes of you,' she said. Mrs. Haggai, it crushed me, and I drew within myself for days and days, like a turtle."

"So, don't you see," Chris told her tactfully, "the real Christina and the Christina you hide behind aren't the same two people. When you're looking after Johnny, that's the real Christina."

Tears came to Christina's eyes, and she became increasingly relaxed as a result of those discussions. When she began coming with questions, my wife knew that rapport had been established and the real Christina was coming into view. But only partly.

Something else seemed to bother her. Something deeper, something she seemed unwilling or unable to share. Chris couldn't put her finger on it at first. Then she noticed, when they went for walks together, Christina preferred to linger about three paces behind. If they met anyone, it was obvious she was being supersensitive about something. But what? "Christina," Chris used to scold her mildly, "I want you to walk up here with me." Chris tried to get her to tell what it was that troubled her. She could see Christina wanted to. At first Chris thought she labored under some deep guilt. Careful questioning, however, revealed nothing to verify that. Then she noticed how, when strangers came, Christina often glanced downward toward her feet.

"O Christina!" my wife exclaimed one day, drawing the Irish girl into her arms. "You're embarrassed about your legs. You have the same problem of so many girls, legs that aren't as attractive as you'd like them to be."

Christina drew away as though Chris had struck her. The eyes of the two women met in intense silence. Only for a moment, though. Then Christina's face began to relax as wonderment came to her countenance. "Ever since I was a child," she whispered, "I've been teased, laughed at . . ."

"Because of your legs!"

She nodded, tears coming to her eyes.

"But what about Johnny?" Chris asked. "How often do we meet people who can't see beyond his physical problems to the real person?"

"That's one of the reasons I love him so," Christina said, the words coming with extreme difficulty. "He teaches me so much—about patience, about acceptance."

"If people look at your legs, if that's all they see," my wife comforted her, "then they're the ones who ought to be embarrassed. Many people are born with physical imperfections. One of the most beautiful people I ever knew was a woman with a terrible birthmark on her face. But she was truly beautiful. Don't you see? It's the inner person that counts. And you're such a beautiful inner person, Christina!"

Christina fairly threw herself into Chris's arms, sobbing. And they talked more and more freely after that, about the extreme legalism among Christians in the community where Christina had grown up, about the emphasis on the things you cannot do as a Christian rather than what you can.

Years later when Chris was with me on one of my

evangelistic crusades, Christina was overheard telling a friend, "I love Mrs. Haggai because she's such a real person. Christians in my community are so withdrawn, so critical. Even our leaders and their wives put you beneath them. But Mrs. Haggai taught me how to live a relaxed and normal Christian life, how to find real happiness in Jesus."

It's not just her husband who appreciates Chris Haggai.

SEVENTEEN

JOHNNY spent most of every twenty-four hours in a prone position, the least taxing posture for his tortured body. He had to be elevated slightly so that the acids from his stomach would not move up the esophagus and cause terrible burning and irritation. One of his problems was that the little trap at the bottom of the esophagus did not close as in a normal body.

So you might think of him as a highly immobile person. Quite the contrary. All I needed to do was to mention some place I would be going, ask if any of the family cared to accompany me, and Johnny's loud "yeah" sounded forth before any of the others could venture an opinion. He could at the moment be very uncomfortable, enduring obvious pain, but however inclement the immediate circumstances, he never turned down an opportunity to sally forth.

Travel with Johnny imposed much extra burden with his daily care schedule. If I planned trips that Chris knew would be too difficult for him, she took care to explain, avoiding disappointment as much as possible.

Part of Johnny's desire for going places stemmed, I'm sure, from the normal traits of childhood. Beyond that, however, a journey, any journey, promised release from what one might call the boredom of inertia. Johnny was not only in the house but confined to just one part of the house unless someone moved him. We looked into wheelchairs that could be self-propelled but found nothing to fit Johnny's special limitations. So we tried to be very tolerant of his yen for travel.

We did considerable travel by automobile since Johnny's needs could best be adapted to that type of travel. When it came time to purchase a new car, little frills and convenient touches received low priority in our family. Would it be comfortable for Johnny? Could his wheelchair fit into the trunk and leave room for other luggage? Those were the prime considerations.

He was a "trouper" when we traveled. I can only wonder, having watched him so often, how it must have both hurt him and elated him to go by car. Hurt him because he saw what an inconvenience he caused. Elated him because the automobile gave him the exhilaration of movement and paraded such a panorama of scenery before his eyes. Yet travel, first and foremost, meant going some place where he would meet new people. Learning about them, he would have new things to think about, new horizons for intercession.

Traveling by car could be quite difficult at times. We needed always to be close to a bathroom, close to running water. At a moment's notice Johnny could become violently ill. But it was worth it all to see joy leap up like fire in his eyes as he heard the thrust of power in an engine and felt the vibrations of movement.

Travel required eating out. Picnics didn't suit our son's limitations, so travel meant restaurants. Fortunately Johnny enjoyed restaurants, even though so little of any menu met his specific needs. He was limited to such bland entries as cooked cereal at breakfast, or soup and apple sauce at other meals. But restaurants meant people to see—even though we made a point of going to meals as late as possible to avoid crowds.

"We prefer a quiet place toward the back," I would tell the hostess, who invariably complied. Waitresses were often thoughtful and accommodating, accepting Johnny as they would any normal person. We have high regard for people in the food service business.

Although he couldn't do justice to the skills of a good chef, Johnny had some memorable restaurant experiences with people. On July 4, 1957, we were in Clarksville, Tennessee, driving toward Mobile, Alabama, for a city-wide meeting in Ladd Stadium. We deliberately selected a hotel with a large dining room so that we could go to a remote corner and cause as little disruption as possible. We also waited until nearly 2:00 p.m., a time when most patrons would have finished their noon meal. We didn't notice a table of three GIs at the extreme opposite end of the dining room. Not until one of them, a young captain, came to our table. He was obviously moved with emotion. His face was flushed, and his eyes were moist. He looked at Johnny and then he looked at me. He loosened his tie, opened his collar button and, while reaching for the chain around his neck on which was a crucifix or a St. Christopher medal (I forget which), he said, "Sir, this has saved my life many times, and I'd like to give it to your little boy."

"Our hope is not in medals, icons, or images, but in the living Lord."

Then with trembling hand and lips quivering, he said, "If you don't mind, sir, if you don't mind."

Good or bad, wise or foolish, I made no further attempt to dissuade him. We all watched with astonishment as this handsome paratrooper tenderly put the chain around Johnny's neck and patted him on the head. Johnny was looking at the young captain with eyes of admiration.

I said, "Son, what's your name?"

"It's all right—" His voice broke off and he strode back across the long dining room where he rejoined his two buddies, went to the cashier, paid the tab for the holiday meal, and they left.

We were all struck completely silent. Our appetites fled. We packed up, paid the cashier, left the restaurant, got into the car, and drove almost all the way to Florence, Alabama, before anyone said a word. That's a little unusual in our group. We are not silent people.

Chris finally broke the brittle atmosphere with "I can't get that young man off my mind."

"Neither can I," said Mother Barker.

"What a stinging rebuke he administers to our own apathy," Chris said.

"What do you mean?" I responded.

"Here was a young man having a Fourth of July holiday meal with two of his buddies. He looked across the large dining room, saw a little boy in great need. The stranger's need elicited his highest compassion. Risking the jeers of his buddies and the rebuffs of the boy's parents, he nevertheless walked across the restaurant and offered to the little stranger what he honestly believed was his most prized possession, what he honestly believed had saved his life on many occasions. He gave that most prized possession to the little boy. Yet we live among many people who need the Lord. They suffer the cerebral palsy of heartbreak, guilt, fear, sin. And we haven't shown as much concern for them as the young captain showed for Johnny. And we know we have the answer. We have not shared our most Prized Possession with them!"

That was a justifiably painful rebuke, and I have never forgotten.

As my appointments became increasingly far-flung, travel had to be by air. You can imagine the excitement the first time we contemplated a plane trip. Mother Barker, Christina, and Chris talked it over at great length, taking care not to let Johnny overhear. Chris tended to be a bit reluctant. "But Johnny would love it. You can be sure of that," Christina offered in her melodious Irish brogue. "I'll look after him when he has trouble. No need for you to put any mind to it at all."

Although we had our apprehensions, the lights all turned green for Johnny at the first mention of a trip by air. He teemed with eagerness as we drove to the airport, chafing at the slightest traffic slowdowns.

He was into his late teens when we took that first trip. We seated him by the window. When the captain announced, "Cleared for takeoff," and those giant engines began their thrust, Johnny's eyes remained riveted to the runway. As we took off he raised his body, as though sensing more than anyone else the buoyant majesty of flight.

He by no means kept his eyes riveted to the window for the entire trip, however. In fact, on every flight we took, beginning with that first air journey, Johnny developed something like a crush on one of the stewardesses—whichever one he considered prettiest and most personable.

It never bothered Johnny, by the way, to arrive at the airport and find a flight delayed. Just wheel his chair off to the side someplace where he could watch the passing throng, and he picked out one young woman after another to follow her graceful movements as she slipped past.

"I'm a sentimental mother, of course," Chris once said. "I admit that. But I don't believe that Johnny, had he been normal like other young men, would have allowed himself to be caught up in the commonplace sexual syndromes of young people today."

One of my staff did considerable study of the current mores among American high-school students and found that a frightening percentage of them now look upon sex as a form of recreation with apparently no moral afterthought. If I thought for a moment that Johnny, with a normal body, might have succumbed to that kind of mentality, then I would most surely have wanted him to be as he was. My heart aches for parents today, especially for Christian parents.

It disturbed us sometimes to see how normal Johnny was mentally in his attitudes toward the opposite sex. Overly romantic scenes on television so upset him, for example, that Chris tried to steer him from such programs. But although he was fully normal, we are confident that he wanted to be as fully moral.

Our assessments of our son, and how he might have been, stem primarily from the friends he chose. He seemed to look for values in people, responding to those values.

He sensed profoundly the deep compassion men like Bob Pierce had for the world's spiritual needs.

He cherished men like Wendell Phillips who understood the world mood and the vision of my ministry to the Third World.

Aunt Bertha of the Children's Bible Hour radio broadcast wrote him lovely letters and Johnny relished every word. He listened to the children's stories on her broadcasts although he generally preferred adult input.

Oral Roberts corresponded with Johnny. Our son expressed strong affection toward Oral and watched many of his telecasts. Johnny was aware of the healing emphasis in Oral's ministry, yet we never felt Johnny emphasized that in his thinking. He seemed willing to accept his physical handicap so that he might exercise his special ministry of prayer.

When Paul Harvey and his lovely wife Angel visited our home, they were delightfully nonchalant with Johnny, chatting about our evangelistic work, about sports, about things in general. On one occasion, when the Harveys came to Atlanta for a speaking engagement, they gave Johnny a special invitation to visit their hotel suite. He treasured such attention. Not because Paul Harvey was a celebrity, but because Johnny liked people who demonstrated meaningful substance in their lives. Paul has a personal charm his fans miss by only seeing or hearing him on his broadcasts.

Johnny especially cherished the visits of Dr. Han. The Korean clergyman is one of the remarkable leaders in the world today, in large part because he never gives the impression of asserting himself. Dr. Han is a man who genuinely exemplifies the power of love in human relations.

It is a mark of respect in Korea to lower your voice when you are in the company of someone you have reason to esteem. I don't think we ever told Johnny that. But tears came to my eyes as Dr. Han pulled his chair up beside Johnny and spoke to him in the soft voice he would use in speaking with his nation's highest leaders. He told our son about the great Young Nak Church and the many people finding Christ through its ministry, and about the growing strength of his country in the face of foreboding threats from the north. He gave Johnny a beautiful sweater which Johnny cherished for the rest of his life.

During one of my 1966 crusades Norma Zimmer was invited as the soloist. It was the first city-wide evangelistic crusade in which she ever participated. Norma was very gracious to Johnny. She had a photograph made of the two of them and frequently sent new record releases to him.

Through my Baltimore crusade Johnny met a number of professional athletes, including Raymond

Berry, possibly the greatest end in football history, and Don Shinnick. After we moved to Atlanta, Felipe Alou of the Atlanta Braves heard about Johnny and sent him an autographed copy of his book, in which Felipe strongly declares himself as a Christian.

But perhaps Johnny's all-time favorite was Jim Irwin. The day Jim took off on his moon flight, Johnny's eyes remained glued to the television screen. For the remainder of his life, Johnny cherished the autograph he received from that famous astronaut. Yet more than anything, Johnny liked the things he heard about Jim's witness and character.

To Chris especially, another meaningful delineation of our son's potential lay in his musical interests. How excited she was to see him discover classical music and especially opera. When Saturday rolled around he wanted to hear the entire radio broadcast of the Metropolitan Opera Company.

In 1966, just before we planned to take Johnny with us on a trip to Hawaii, he began to suffer acutely from a hiatal hernia. Because of Johnny's breathing problems, the doctors prescribed surgery. His eyes filled with anguish at the news.

"Okay, Johnny," I told him, "if you do well, we'll go to Hawaii for a few days."

The prospect changed his whole attitude toward the surgery. We got some airline posters and displayed them all over his room. Chris read to him from travel promotion folders. Johnny rose to the occasion with an attitude of raw determination. The trip turned out to be ideal for convalescence and morale building. Hawaii's climate, we discovered, agreed with Johnny more than any other place we had ever taken him. We went to the International Marketplace, to the Kodak show, and for long and leisurely forays on the beach.

One night our dear friend Wendell Phillips invited us to the Kahala Hilton to see the delightful Danny Kalakini show. It was during the Viet Nam War, with many servicemen on "R & R" thronging the place along with the tourists. During intermission, Wendell got a sudden inspiration and stood to his feet. "I want all of you people to meet my friend!" he called out. "He's as brave as any soldier. He has fought battles the rest of us know nothing about, never complaining or feeling sorry for himself. He can't stand up because he's in a wheelchair. If you stretch a bit, maybe you can see him. He's my dear friend, Johnny Haggai."

The audience exploded into applause. GIs cheered. And Johnny grinned his entire full face. He became second billing that night and thrived on it.

After we established headquarters in Atlanta, we frequently took Johnny to Stone Mountain, a nearby family amusement park. We also took him to the Georgia State Fair. He was game to ride on everything from the tilt-a-whirl to the merry-go-round. Of course, only a few rides were really adapted to his circumstances. He understood. He relished every moment and was ready at the first glimpse of a ticket to go again and again.

So, as with any young man, there were many hues to Johnny's interests. The most pronounced evidence of his values lay in his identification with our ministry, particularly in the Third World. One day

I asked Chris, "Do you think Johnny could take a trip all the way to Singapore?"

Common sense and maternal instinct should have evoked a resounding "No!" But after some sober thought she said, "Do you think he could take it?"

"I don't know. But I'm sure he needs the experience."

We gave the suggestion days of thought and much prayer. We consulted Johnny's doctor. We talked to members of our team to ask if they thought such a trip might in any way impose upon the effectiveness of the work. Everything turned up positive.

We called the local Pan American office and told them about Johnny's situation. "We've taken many paraplegics on board our planes," they said. "If you have someone along to look after your son, to be fully responsible for him, you'll find that our flight crews will do everything they can to make him comfortable." That settled it.

My colleagues had organized a mission tour of some twenty-five Americans, ministers and laity, and I took special care that Johnny would not impose inconvenience upon any of them. In fact, we flew on separate flights most of the trip. They, however, all took to Johnny with warmth and enthusiasm. He became the official mascot.

Once we got to Singapore, however, once he met all those Institute delegates from Asia and Africa, Johnny all but forgot about the American entourage. He wanted to be at the training sessions at the Hotel Singapura, listen to the lectures, hear the men talk about their countries and their ministries.

The Third World became almost an obsession with Johnny. He cherished objects, however small, if he knew the origin to be some place in Africa, the Middle East, or Asia. When reports from such countries appeared on television, he begged to be wheeled close to the set so as not to miss the smallest detail.

The war in Viet Nam disturbed him deeply as did the bloodshed in other areas of Southeast Asia. The word *communism* became anathema to him, for he clearly understood the threat posed by Marxist communism to the cause of evangelism throughout Asia. His life became saturated with interest in and concern for the Third World. I doubt that anyone ever prayed more for the Third World than Johnny did.

"Christians are so calloused sometimes," I would say to him. "I don't know how to get them to see the opportunities we have in the world today."

But Johnny saw. Had he himself been permitted a normal existence, I doubt that anyone else could have so eloquently sounded forth the message.

EIGHTEEN

JOHNNY was one of the most sanguine persons I have ever known. In spite of moods, frustration, and much pain, he was amazingly resilient. I like to believe he experienced many intervals of release as his mind gave itself completely to happy thoughts. He indicated that in many ways, especially with his sense of humor.

How good God was to spare his capacity for laughter from the crippling nemesis that laid waste to most of his physical capacities. Even in times of great pain or discomfort, he could see or hear something amusing and manage a radiant smile—or even burst into audible laughter. My, how he could laugh—from the top of his head to the tip of his toes. He often shook with laughter, laughing so hard that tears streamed down his cheeks.

Chris tends by nature to be rather serious—though she enjoys good humor and on occasion can bowl you over with a hilarious insight. Again and again Johnny unknowingly ministered to her in her need for an emotional lift. Life imposes demands and hardships upon all people, on some more than others, but if we can nurture an honest sense of humor we can reduce the magnitude of many problems.

The older Johnny got, the more we saw his debility as a circumstance rather than a handicap. I believe that God endows everyone with the physical and mental traits needed to perform his will for that individual's life. Who can be sure that with a healthy body Johnny would have served God more effectively than he actually did? Human nature, even among supposedly committed people, tends to think of health as license for personal and materialistic activity rather than for complete investment of strength and talent and time in selfless service for our Lord.

I know that many times Johnny longed for a normal body, or at least a more normal one. But his sense of humor demonstrated both that he accepted his lot in life and that he really did put the will of God above normal human wants. Very little of his life could be considered normal. We had his bathroom rigged with pulleys and trolleys and all sorts of contraptions to help manipulate him more effectively. Instead of seeing those devices as further extensions of his handicap, however, he enjoyed them.

"Time for today's circus performance," Christina might say as she wheeled him in for his bath. "Are we going to swing on the high trapeze or walk the tight wire?"

We called his area in the house the bachelor pad. He slept in a fully equipped hospital bed. But he preferred for us to call it the executive bed.

He looked for excuses to joke with Chris and turned many a dull and demanding day into smiles as they teased each other. As you realize, they had some very difficult days. Because she so staunchly refused to pamper him, a situation he sometimes protested but I know appreciated, they did not always enjoy flawless rapport.

"You know," she said one time, "you need to trade off this mother and get a better one."

"Yeah!" he agreed, obviously struggling to appear serious and prevent a smile from spreading full across his face.

"Well, now," his mother continued, "maybe I can help you. Would you like me to call the mothers' bureau and have them send you another mother?"

Silence.

She pressed the issue lightly, asking, "I'm sure they could send you a good one. Would you like a blond mother, a red head, or a brunette? You like brunettes."

By that time he could suppress his mirth no longer, no matter how uncomfortable he felt.

"Of course, Johnny," Chris teased, "if we run an ad for another mother, we must tell the truth about her son. He becomes very grumpy and uncooperative sometimes."

One day she asked Johnny if he would like to go shopping with her, the type of invitation he never turned down. I was in the house at the time and casually joked, "Say, Johnny, I wonder if you'd be my representative. Don't let your mother spend any

199

money." Chris joined in on the bantering, never realizing what the end result would be. When they got to the store, she set out immediately to purchase a few things she had wanted for some time but just hadn't gotten to. Johnny looked on soberly. When she selected some gloves and went to the counter to pay for them, he set to howling as though he had been stuck with a pin.

"Quiet, Johnny," Chris reprimanded, attempting once more to consummate the purchase.

But he protested all the louder. Johnny could be extremely vocal, which some people interpreted as a form of mental retardation. Not in the least. It seems he so fully accepted his physical deformity, learning to tolerate the unkind and curious eyes often fixed upon him, that he could also accept his inability to speak and would let out with sounds rather unacceptable to those who didn't understand. He called upon his full range of groans and growls that day and left his mother with no recourse but to abandon the purchase and wheel him out of the store.

"Don't you ever do a thing like that again," she lamented after they returned home.

Johnny didn't pick on his mother to the exclusion of others. He enjoyed every bit as much pulling a joke on me.

Before we launched our Third World ministry, we held a crusade in Baton Rouge. What a joy it was to see thousands of people throng to the big ten-thousand seat tent night after night. We took Johnny. You would have thought he was the evangelist. He was very fussy about what he wore every night and wanted to be sure we arrived well ahead of the opening song.

The last two nights we moved to an outdoor stadium, which Johnny especially enjoyed. It was built to fit the contour of the land, so that when people came from the parking lot, they entered from the top of the bleachers. That intrigued Johnny.

Of course, crusades of such magnitude necessarily required a lot of money. At times they became targets for criticism, with the evangelist the "bull's eye" at the heart of the target. I strove for impeccable integrity in the handling of money, insisting that every detail of a crusade be carefully budgeted. In fact, I preferred not to mention money at all. But many people think God has given me a special gift for raising funds to support worthy causes, so when offerings lagged behind the budget of a crusade I would sometimes acquiesce to the local committee's urging and present the offering appeal. Such was the situation one night at Baton Rouge.

I didn't go into detail about my careful fiscal philosophy, but I told the people how much the budget was and how far we were running short of that budget. Then I said, "It's unfortunate we've had the occasional Elmer Gantry in evangelism. Such people make it difficult for those who do operate with integrity. Some people say we're in evangelism for the money we get out of it."

At the top of his voice Johnny hollered "Yeah!" I was struck silent, as was the audience. Then the crowd realized who had made the taunt and burst into loud laughter. Johnny became an instant celebrity and we received one of the finest offerings ever to gladden a local committee. Of course, not a cent of it went to me.

I once held a crusade for Bill Smith, a dear pastor friend of many years. I seldom took individual church meetings, but that one was different. It was in Honolulu, and Johnny loved Hawaii.

One night Bill got up and said, "Tonight we're going to take an offering for our evangelist and his family." Caught by surprise, I became very uneasy. "Now," Bill continued, "Dr. Haggai doesn't really approve of this." In jest he continued, "Well, if our evangelist won't take the offering, perhaps we can find someone else who will."

"Yeah!" Johnny cried out.

Johnny's timing was perfect. He knew that if he vocalized too often he would offend people. So, like a skilled comedian, he carefully interposed himself at strategic moments. Some people didn't understand, but most did.

One night at the Baton Rouge crusade mentioned earlier, Eddie Nicholson was leading the singing. He began recognizing people who had come from long distances.

First he called out nearby cities and areas in Louisiana, then proceeded to Texas.

"Are other states represented?" he asked.

No one responded, though I'm sure there were some.

No one responded, that is, except Johnny, who called out, "Yeah! Yeah!"

"Oh, yes," Eddie said, "we forgot Johnny Haggai here. He comes from Atlanta, Georgia."

"Yeah!" our son fairly bellowed.

Johnny and Christina often joked with each other about such things as her cooking. For instance, Mother Barker made a very tasty custard. One day Christina tried the recipe with considerable success, but Johnny wouldn't admit her custard was good. He acted as if it were unfit for human consumption.

"Wigs on the green, Johnny!" Christina chided, using an Irish term for challenging a fight. "Going on at me, that way!"

Johnny frowned.

She put her hands to her hips, cocked her head, and said, "I'm fell out with you for just one hour!"

Johnny smiled, then resumed the frown.

"For just a minute then," she consoled, "and the minute is right now over."

Whereupon Johnny ate the dessert with gusto.

Johnny could dish it out, but he could also take a joke on himself. He had a very dear friend, a black woman by the name of Hattie. During one visit to her home, he sat listening to some Paul Whiteman music on the radio. Johnny liked rhythm and began keeping time by bumping his shoe against the metal plate on his chair.

Hattie came to him and, feigning complete seriousness, pretended to scold, "Aren't you ashamed of yourself, young man, dancing while your father is out trying to win souls?"

Johnny laughed. And whenever he was with Hattie after that, he always did his little routine and she always responded by "scolding" him.

During one crusade to which Chris brought Johnny, song leader Felix Snipes brought his pretty wife Patsy and their eight-month-old son. Johnny spent hours of each day in or around the motel swimming pool, and both Felix and Patsy became very friendly with him. Felix and I were away one afternoon when Mother Barker asked Chris to take her shopping for a few moments. Chris didn't want to leave Johnny, but it was a chore getting him in and out of the car.

"Why not just leave him with me?" Patsy offered. "I'll need a bodyguard here all by myself."

Johnny's eyes sparkled.

"I've had enough sun for today," Patsy said. "Why not roll Johnny into my room and I'll just sit with him there while you're gone?"

Felix and I returned before Mother Barker and Chris did. I went to our room, Felix to his.

"Now look here, young man!" Felix called out in a gruff voice as he opened the door. "What are you doing in this room with my wife?"

Johnny never forgot the fun of that moment. Every time Felix saw him after that, he would tease Johnny about "trying to steal his wife away from him."

Johnny was full of the joy of life. No wonder we miss that dear boy so. He wanted personal happiness the same as anyone. But I think he most enjoyed contributing to the happiness of others.

Our son clung to his own possessions. If he owned a pencil, which he could never use, he still wouldn't give it to anyone. But money was different. I think if he'd been a millionaire, he might have given it all away. He loved to use his money to buy gifts for others. Christina would take him shopping for his mother's birthday and Chris would take him for Christina's and mine and Mother Barker's.

Johnny was an astute shopper. Christina remembers taking him to shop for a gift for his mother. He decided on earrings. Chris hadn't been aware of his noticing, for she didn't wear them very often. "It was amazing," Christina related, "what he knows about jewelry. The clerk wasn't very helpful at first. I suppose she thought she could bring out ordinary costume jewelry and Johnny'd not know the difference. But he soon enough set her straight on that."

Because it fascinated him so to buy gifts for us, he found it difficult to keep those gifts secret. He not only wavered with the secrecy of his own acquisitions but he wasn't the best person to share secrets with concerning gifts one of us purchased for another family member. One Christmas his mother bought a new watch for me. She found it on sale in November and couldn't resist the purchase. Nor could she resist showing it to Johnny. "But you must keep it a complete secret," she cautioned.

"Yeah!" Johnny agreed.

"We mustn't say a word of it to Daddy."

Give Johnny a high mark for effort. He really tried. But as Chris presumed he would, he quickly let me know there was a secret. She didn't mind, knowing how much joy it would give Johnny to tease me about knowing something I didn't know.

"Is it something I'm to wear?" I asked.

Johnny laughed.

"Well, if it's something I wear, is it for lounging around the house or for use when I'm away?"

Again Johnny laughed.

"Maybe it doesn't involve clothes at all, is that right?"

"Yeah!"

"Is it something for the car?" For my office?"

Only laughter.

Then one night, one rare such occasion, we sat as a family watching television. Wouldn't you know, one of the commercials advertised Omega watches! Johnny grew tense. Chris looked at him, smiled softly, and—since I was intently watching the screen —cautiously shook her head.

Johnny smiled back. He meant to keep the secret. But as part of the commercial, the very model Chris had purchased for me appeared in a full closeup on the television screen. Johnny gave a big lurch. It was the kind of movement he had reserved as his response to very personal and important situations, and we all knew it. I turned immediately to Johnny, looked back at the screen, and then to Johnny again.

"A watch?" I questioned cautiously.

Again Johnny tried not to give it away.

"I'm getting a watch for Christmas, is that it?"

Unable to contain the secret any longer, Johnny responded with an enthusiastic "Yeah! Yeah!"

Johnny relished slapstick. Pie in the face and slippery banana peelings were undoubtedly prime props in his imaginary bag of tricks.

He cracked up whenever I told him about an incident at my father's first church in Middleville, Michigan. One of the members, who had both a wooden leg and false teeth came one sultry afternoon to a funeral in the sanctuary. As he squeezed into a pew a little dog ventured up as far as the church doorway, which had been open for ventilation.

Just as the service got underway, the man with the wooden leg gave out a thundering sneeze. He sneezed so violently that his uppers sailed out and landed in the aisle. At that the dog came bounding in and snapped up the dentures before they had scarcely come to rest.

Johnny would roar with laughter at the bizarre scene of the man scrambling about the sanctuary on his wooden leg trying to catch the dog and retrieve his uppers, while my father stared in amazement from the pulpit.

Once when my cousin Leo visited, he went to great lengths about how cruel I was for not providing Johnny with a better wheelchair. "Why, Johnny," Leo said, "they've got these things motorized with reclining backs, windshield wipers, air conditioning, and ejector seats." The more eloquent Leo waxed, the better Johnny liked it.

One time when he was especially distraught about my leaving on an extended overseas trip, I appealed to Johnny's sense of humor.

"You have a ball whenever I come back, don't you?" I asked.

"Yeah!" he admitted.

"Well," I continued, "how can you enjoy having me come back if I don't go away?"

That was one of the few times Johnny was smiling as I left on a trip.

NINETEEN

FOR ALL THE JOY Johnny gave us, the most profound dimensions of human pain permeated his own existence. Among those was the pain of frustration, which far exceeded physical disability. Johnny, in fact, really didn't think of himself as handicapped. In one of our earlier endeavors to help him, we took him to a school for children suffering from cerebral palsy. He became very puzzled, first looking at us and then at the children as if to ask, "Why on earth did you bring me to a place like this? What's the matter with these kids?" It would have displeased him if we had chosen some similarly handicapped person as a playmate. He grew restless at the sight of even one such person. His own wheelchair he could accept, but place him in a surrounding of wheelchairs and he became downright uncooperative.

It was the onslaught of frustration, resulting from his handicap, with which he could never adequately cope. People talk about having knots in their stomachs when things don't go right. Johnny was like a boiling volcano inside. He didn't just want to walk, he wanted to play football. He didn't just want to reach out his hand and touch, he wanted to express himself with a typewriter. He didn't just want to talk, he wanted to proclaim the glory of God's salvation.

He had an incredibly long attention span. Once he got something on his mind it stayed there until he saw it resolved.

Think back to the last time you tried to explain something, perhaps a new program for your church or civic organization. The concept was crystal clear in your own mind. If only your associates could see what you saw, the project could have been effectively expedited. But for some reason you just couldn't get across what you envisioned. That sort of frustration was a round-the-clock nightmare for Johnny.

We prayed for wisdom, imploring God to give us some kind of living link with Johnny's mind. I believe scientists haven't yet begun to discover the wonders of the human brain, that greatest of all computers, our Creator's masterpiece. Perhaps some day an instrument will be developed, sensitive to the emanation of brain waves so that unfortunates like Johnny can make known their thoughts, their reactions and needs and desires, their pain and pleasure. I'm not talking about contemporary mysticism or the exploration of the occult. I simply believe that God has placed laws and capabilities in his creation that we have yet to discover.

Our adeptness for communication with Johnny did improve through the years.

"Chris," Mother Barker would call out, "see if you can understand what he wants."

And, sometimes the reverse was true. That situation occurred many times. And, thank God, Chris often understood. She was marvelously sensitive to him. Christina became very responsive too, to his wants and needs. But often, much too often, we didn't understand. And it frustrated him all the more in proportion to the importance of what he wanted to tell us. He would try to get something across and when we didn't understand, consternation etched more and more deeply across his face.

"Did it happen today?" Chris might ask.

If it didn't, Johnny would grunt negative response.

"Was it yesterday?"

It wasn't.

"Does it have something to do with our trip last month? A place where we stopped? Someone you saw? Something we did?"

Wrong.

At times we would seem to come close to the subject. His eyes would brighten then and our hearts quicken with anticipation. But with disturbing frequency we would have to say, "Johnny, we're so sorry, but we just can't understand."

After that he would sit, at times for hours, in contemplative disappointment. Sometimes his depression deepened to such an extent we feared he might never snap out of it. I'm convinced it was not merely a role he played, a ploy for sympathy.

After I resigned from the pastorate and especially

after we formed Haggai Institute, which required so many extended assignments out of the country, Johnny missed me tremendously. He fell into some moods from which he wouldn't fully recover until the moment the door opened and he recognized my footsteps.

"This is the first he's brightened up since you left," Chris told me one time.

I sometimes wondered if it would have been better if his hearing hadn't been so alert. "I declare," Christina told him, "you can hear the grass grow!" Like a watchdog, he never missed a sound around the house. If some strange noise occurred and we could define it, we always told him. He knew when the mail arrived. He detected the arrival of the men who came to read the meters, differentiating between the man from the gas company and the ones who checked water and electricity. If the phone rang he listened intently to the conversation. Whenever we needed to talk about things he ought not to hear, we retired to another room and whispered. And the whispers dared not be more than scarcely audible to us.

From earliest childhood he wanted to walk. If we would manipulate his little feet as though in ambulatory movement, he would laugh so hard that we might have to put him back into his crib. The first time he saw someone use crutches, after he had begun to learn the dimensions of his own limitations, his eyes sparkled as his alert mind began to imagine all sorts of applications he might give to such a wondrous facility.

Because he so wanted to participate with the world around him we constantly looked for alternatives.

When he was younger, for example, and his mother vacuumed the floor, she would move his wheelchair with one hand and the vacuum with the other, placing his little hand on the handle so he would seem to be performing the household chore with her.

Life granted him few respites, but one was dreams. When as a young child he napped, my wife frequently came by his crib and found him asleep with a broad smile on his lips. That subconscious facility apparently developed as he grew older. What wonders sleep must have held for him, and what frustration awakening must have been.

We had no way of accurately assessing his imagination. We can only assume that, because of his enormous curiosity, his innate capability for remembering details, he possessed a vivid imagination. Because of that, I think life also granted him the respite of vicarious experience during his hours awake.

He was an avid sports fan. And what man or boy goes to a football game without seeing himself as the quarterback throwing a touchdown pass or as a lineman stopping a big play? Johnny was an enthusiastic spectator. Had it not been for television, which he preferred because it didn't require leaving the small comforts provided at home, I'm sure he would have insisted we take him to sporting events as often as we could spare the time.

He especially enjoyed basketball. His favorite team was the Harlem Globetrotters. Meadowlark Lemon would send him into convulsions of laughter. I wish we could have arranged for him to meet that famous basketball team.

He tolerated baseball, Mother Barker's favorite sport, and no matter what team she rooted for, he picked the opposite. He gloated and preened, amused to his very marrow whenever her team lost and his won (however sparse his real loyalty for the winning team may have been).

It concerned me many times to realize how fully he identified with what he saw on television. You could almost see him moving down the basketball floor on a fast break, falling back for a jump shot, driving in to get a rebound. He played the full game, never once allowing himself a moment's rest on the bench. We occasionally had to bring a towel to wipe the perspiration from his face, he worked so hard during a game. More than once he became ill because he got so tense watching, but we always felt it was worth it.

One Saturday afternoon he and Chris watched a televised basketball game between paraplegics. Who knows what went through his mind? That was something completely new. Chris tried to make use of the situation by saying, "That's a good illustration of how people who are handicapped in one way but not in others can overcome their handicap somewhat. Of course, there are many, many handicapped people who at one time could have played basketball just like a regular athlete but who wouldn't be able to participate in the game you are seeing now." Johnny never really identified with what he saw on the screen that afternoon, not at all in the way he did with games among normal athletes, and Chris finally diverted his attention and turned off the set.

"Do you suppose Johnny might enjoy bowling?" I asked one time.

Chris hesitated, knowing well how it frustrated

Johnny to want to participate in everything. Yet against her better judgment, she said, "We could try."

Johnny howled his approval at the idea.

At the recreation center I carefully fitted his fingers into the bowling ball, supported his arm and moved it back, then let the ball go. Down the alley it went, knocking over several pins.

"Yeah! Yeah!" Johnny exclaimed.

Early one evening as we got in some bowling before the teams arrived, a man came up to us. "I've been here several times when you've brought your son," he said. "I wonder if you'd let me have some pictures taken so I can write a little story. I'm a reporter for the *Constitution*." We refused. Johnny didn't approve the decision, but he understood. We simply couldn't bring ourselves to any action that might be interpreted as using Johnny's infirmity to soften people's hearts toward my ministry.

(Unfortunately, a common procedure in many fund-raising programs is to ask, "What's our 'orphan' here?" In other words, what will touch emotional sympathies enough to reach pocketbooks? I am determined to stay with the facts in fund raising for the Haggai Institute. It takes hundreds of thousands of dollars to run such a program, reaching out to residents of the Third World, yet many people will give to spiritual causes only if human infirmity is somehow involved.)

Much as Johnny wanted to talk, to walk, to participate, I think he was most frustrated by the insurmountable wall his handicap placed between him and the opposite sex. Johnny was a ladies' man. In spite of his disastrous inadequacy of muscle tissue, he seemed to be well endowed with testosterone, the androgenic hormone that produces masculinity. But his circumstances forced him continually to sublimate his feelings toward girls.

Before his teens, when we still lived in Louisville, I hired a young woman home from college for the summer to do secretarial work at the house. She was a lovely girl with sparkling eyes and flowing blond hair. As we always did when strangers came to the house, we introduced her to Johnny. He was infatuated at first sight. She detected the fact, as did we, and was a good sport about it.

"Do you mind if I wheel him here to your doorway?" Chris asked, when after two days Johnny couldn't keep his eyes off the door to the room where she worked.

"Let him come on inside here with me," she said. Johnny almost swooned. The joy of every day that summer became finishing breakfast, getting cleaned and dressed, and then waiting for that wisp of loveliness to arrive. Johnny never took his eyes off her from the moment she began typing until she cheerfully departed. It was one of his best summers. When she returned to college in the fall, Johnny fell into a chronic melancholy that lasted for days.

Johnny's preference for adults extended to members of the opposite sex, but there were exceptions. His first serious love among his peers was a pretty girl named Patty. May God ever enrich her life for her patience and loveliness to him! She talked to him, asked him questions about his interests and, if we had recently taken a trip, about his activities. In the short time they knew each other she learned to communicate with him quite well and Johnny adored her for it. She was like a modern Psyche, the mythical maiden with whom Cupid was said to have fallen in love. Lithe of movement, with a full and dainty figure, she became the wonder of Johnny's eyes. I suppose some parents might have mildly reprimanded him. We didn't.

I think Johnny formed in his mind an ideal for womanhood and, had he been normal, he would have blessed some young woman's life with loving patience and attention. He saw every charming female as an embodiment of at least some aspect of that total ideal.

In later years he developed a deep infatuation for one of the women at Haggai Institute headquarters. She was gracious and understanding, and would hold his hand and talk to him about happenings of the day and aspects of our ministry. At first we teased him. But when we saw how deeply he felt about her, we quietly agreed among ourselves to stop doing that.

While living in Louisville, I had my office at home. I frequently relied on temporary talent from downtown employment agencies to provide additional secretarial work when the load was heavier than usual. The fact that a number of young women came in and out of our house got to be an adventure for Johnny. He would wonder whether or not he would approve of a new secretary coming for work.

On one occasion, Chris jokingly said to Johnny, "If the girl coming this morning is ugly, she can stay; if she is pretty, out she goes."

"Yeah," he agreed.

Well, the young lady came. Johnny sat like a judge

at the Miss America Pageant when the door opened and the new recruit was ushered in. Well, her personal grooming left much to be desired. She wore a wrinkled dress. Her hair looked as though it hadn't been fixed in days, and she had a run in her hose. Johnny went into almost uncontrollable laughter. Chris said she was so afraid that on that one occasion he was going to break forth into audible speech and embarrass us all.

"So she can stay?" his mother whispered.

"Yeah," Johnny responded loudly.

TWENTY

THANK GOD, there was much joy in Johnny's life. Yet I wonder if his sense of humor wasn't uniquely related to the depths of his pain. Philosophers tell us that only the thinnest demarcation separates pain from laughter, levity from tragedy. It could be that his bubbling sense of humor stemmed directly from his pain and frustration. It was his way of saying he had come to terms with his own personal reality and circumstances.

Johnny had a message for people—for those who are lonely, misunderstood, frustrated. A message of love to people who can't see beyond a person's skin, who miss the wealth of discovering that life's greatest beauty can sometimes be found in what seems to be life's greatest ugliness.

Johnny's favorite song was "How Great Thou Art." "Stand up for Jesus" was a close second. He didn't like "Abide With Me." I'm not sure why, perhaps because it suggested the foreboding likelihood of his own short life span. Whenever he heard it, sadness covered his face.

He was deeply sensitive to spiritual things. "Do you think the Lord would be pleased, Johnny?" was all we had to ask if something questionable arose—and that usually closed the subject.

I once discussed with him how struggle builds character, going into considerable detail about what our affluent society does to the human mind by letting everything come so easy to many people. We talked about how the satisfying of carnal desires can lower the frustration threshold of people. They can sink more and more deeply until they develop mental illness or even commit suicide.

But back to Johnny's tastes in music. During the days of my city-wide crusades, my wife sometimes sang "I've Discovered the Way of Gladness" as a duet with a male vocalist. That became Johnny's all-time favorite special number. Once while taking care of him, Chris began humming the tune. To the best of his ability Johnny tried to hum along with her. He couldn't carry a tune but he could certainly make "a joyful noise," as the Bible says.

On an impulse Chris burst into singing the song as she had done in the duets. Johnny was elated and took over the male part.

"I've discovered the way of gladness," his mother sang.

Then, fortissimo, Johnny came in with his inar-

ticulate voicing of "I've discovered the way of joy."
Exactly eight syllables, as in the song.

"I've discovered relief from sadness."

"'Tis a happiness without alloy."

Gibberish? That would have been the assessment of some. But Chris knew that Johnny was encoding every word, as clearly as any vocalist ever did, although his manacled tongue could articulate only a quagmire of apparently meaningless noise.

Even in days of deepest pain Johnny loved to sing. Don't tell me that a boy who relished opera and symphony couldn't understand how music reaches up and praises the Lord. Don't tell me he didn't understand the ministry of music, the message that God-honoring lyrics can express. Johnny was message oriented. Sing "Sweet Hour of Prayer," and that's just what he wanted to do, pray. Sing "Love Lifted Me," and a glow of spiritual joy came to his eyes. He thrilled to songs about love and peace and assurance.

So that's the *why* of this book, to help Johnny speak out—about love, about meaning in life, about understanding C. S. Lewis's words: "Pain can be God's megaphone to awaken a deaf world."

To husbands and wives struggling to keep a marriage together, Johnny would cry out, "Love!" Find the value in each other. See more than the mirror sees, more than the scale reveals. See what God sees, what is deep inside waiting to radiate like the dawn if we will only search out the full constellation of just one divinely created person. For that's what we are, you know, every one of us—intricately and purposefully designed by our Creator.

Johnny was so designed: a gallant in disguise, a preacher unable to deliver one word of a sermon, a singer whose songs were locked up in a soul bursting with music.

I don't understand pain. Socrates believed that the sublime could be found only through suffering. I treasure our Lord's promise in the book of Romans, so aptly paraphrased in the Living Bible: "But if we are to share his glory, we must also share his suffering. Yet what we suffer now is nothing compared to the glory he will give us later."

I want with all my heart to be Johnny's voice in proclaiming to you how eternally meaningful suffering can be. But let me put on the record how much I respected our son for his attitude, his acceptance of what had to be. Johnny was a hero, as much as any soldier who ever marched, any athlete who displayed prowess above the highest efforts of others. I pay tribute to him not as my son but as a truly noble person who hovered in the shadows but dared to face life as though he walked in the sunshine. I doubt if he ever had a fully comfortable moment, even in sleep, yet he rarely complained. We are so much the better people for having spent twenty-four years in close relationship to him.

I think back to when we first brought him home from the hospital. He could take only liquid. Even a few trickles created terrible agony for him. Many days, during his earliest infancy, we expected certain death. But somehow, no matter how deep he sank, he revived.

Then around Christmastime and on into January,

he began to improve. He put on some weight. His eyes brightened ever so little. Deep in my heart I wanted to think he might be a normal boy after all.

Johnny had extreme difficulty breathing those first months. Our pediatrician suggested we take him to a throat specialist who, in turn, recommended a tracheotomy. Chris suddered at the thought of it and asked to see another doctor. The second doctor prescribed a vapor tent, giving Chris medication to use with it.

In four hours Johnny's breathing problem, characterized by a shrill whisper, disappeared. But then he developed terrible congestion, and we thought we would lose him. Yet he clung to life—clung, I now believe, to his destiny.

He didn't like the darkness of the little tent so we placed a small light inside. That didn't fully satisfy him either. So Chris would spend an hour or more at a time with her head under the tent, talking to him, humming, stroking him. He never consciously recognized her presence. But if she drew away while he was still awake, he fretted.

My wife devotedly maintained a tireless vigil those early months. Only God knows what significant contributions she made to Johnny's life by insisting upon giving him her fullest concern. All recognize the importance of a mother's love, her reassuring voice, in the earliest stages of childhood. I suspect that Johnny was as responsive and perceptive as any infant. It was just that at first he had complete inability to evidence response.

I can't say exactly when Chris fully accepted the

fact of Johnny's lifetime prognosis. What I want to emphasize is the complete validity of two of God's promises. They were valid for my wife and valid for Johnny.

The first: "We know that all things work together for good to them that love God" (Romans 8:28).

The second: "The joy of the Lord is your strength" (Nehemiah 8:10).

Promises such as those sustained Chris over and over through the years. Her role in motherhood was certainly not the usual one, but she is convinced that there are multitudes of mothers who would have responded to a child's misfortune just as she did toward our child.

So my relating of Johnny's story becomes not so much our experience as an illustration of how parents can find joy in even the most adverse circumstances. For love is the greatest power known to humankind. We can experience that power only in direct relationship to the circumstances in which we exercise it. For those whose "Johnny experience" may lie in the future, I hope that sharing our experience may help to provide fortification and encouragement.

Johnny was a great illustration to me of God's relationship to his children. The greater our need, the more abundant his supply of strength and grace and mercy. I have no doubt that we spent three times the amount of money on Johnny that an average family spends on one normal child. And Chris, Mother Barker, and Christina—with occasional assists from me—devoted ten times and more the hours, even after his teens. It was not that we loved him more than other parents love their offspring, but rather that his need was greater.

So, especially as I saw my wife's unselfish care and concern for Johnny, I did a good bit of thinking about how we confuse things as Christians. We heap attention upon the spiritually robust and give the least attention to those with the greatest spiritual need.

For all Johnny's disability, he was the farthest thing from a hypochondriac. He relished good health, however small the morsels of it may have been. If he sniffled a bit and we mentioned the possibility of his catching cold, he could become highly irritated. We had to be very careful of colds, because he suffered from almost continual respiratory difficulties. Even the slightest infection could bring him to the brink of death. Chris was very careful to avoid bringing people with colds into his presence.

Once a husband and wife from Indonesia visited our home and Johnny went with Chris to the airport to meet them. She presumed he would throw open the widest doors of his heart to such visitors from the Third World. On the contrary, he rejected them. As they came in from the baggage claim area, Chris tried to introduce him to them. To her surprise and embarrassment, he turned away. Then the wife sneezed and Chris understood. She hadn't noticed that the visitor was suffering rather badly from a cold. But Johnny had.

The last two or three years of his life he endured constant pain, day and night. He would look up at us, wide vistas of hurt so obvious in his eyes, and quietly mumble, "Umn, umn, umn."

"Pain?" his mother would ask.

"Yeah!"

Sometimes she could determine where the pain was and try to give him some relief. Other times she would ask many questions but be unable to isolate the specific area of his suffering.

He had a chronic intestinal problem, a kind of constriction that gave him increased discomfort during the final years. "It can be as painful as kidney stones," his doctor told us, "as painful as childbirth."

"And there's no medication?" I asked.

"There is," the doctor replied, "but to administer it to Johnny would be fatal." The medication would inhibit peristalsis, numbing the function of the intestines to remove body waste. Even a healthy body could only briefly tolerate such a buildup of toxic content.

Johnny had to be hospitalized frequently. One time, just a year before he left us, not only was he sick in the hospital with internal pain but sores had developed in his mouth. Chris remembers coming to the room and seeing Mother Barker stooped over him, Johnny's mouth opened wide, as she tenderly massaged the sores. Chris could only partially hold back her tears on seeing such a beautiful expression of love.

The year we took Johnny to Singapore he suffered terrific discomfort. One of the hotel maids became especially concerned and ventured the shy suggestion that we ought to try acupuncture. When we expressed some interest, she began describing friends of hers who had suffered from various maladies and had been helped by practioners in her city. Both of us tended to be skeptical. A few months later when I was in Korea, my friend Mr. Cha Il Suk, president of the Chosen Hotel Corporation, told me about a Dr. Kim who had just migrated to America and was based at a rehabilitation center in New Jersey.

"Dr. Kim is one of the world's foremost acupuncture specialists," Mr. Cha said. Dr. Kim's services, however, came only at an extremely high fee. Nevertheless, after Chris and I had talked about the matter, we decided to call him to see if he might possibly come to Atlanta and have a look at our son. He agreed. At a cost of one thousand dollars.

We went to great length explaining the procedure to Johnny, and his enthusiasm grew the more we told him.

A look of great anticipation came to Johnny's eyes as Dr. Kim stepped up to him. To our dismay the doctor gave only a superficial checkup.

"What would it cost to have you proceed with treatment?" I asked.

"With your travel, hotel costs, and all, it could be between seventy-five and hundred thousand dollars a year," the doctor told us. "I can't promise the results. We may be able to help your son's speech. It's possible he may improve sufficiently to roll his chair by himself."

We discussed it carefully with Johny. "A hundred thousand dollars is completely beyond our reach," we told him.

"Yeah," Johnny agreed in quiet resignation.

TWENTY-ONE

WE HAVE been able to establish a kind of South Pacific second front for the Haggai Institute work. At the outset, that excited Johnny very much. He became nearly as interested in the continent "down under" as in the Third World. And Australia does have a unique geographical kinship to the Third World.

I almost never conduct crusades anymore, and never in North America, but the mass meeting approach was advised by our Australian friends as ideal for establishing a base on which to build our larger ministry. So in 1971 I was asked to meet with some leaders in Australia for the purpose of future planning. Johnny and Chris accompanied me.

Johnny all but flew that plane himself across the

Pacific. He didn't even want to linger in Hawaii.

He did better when traveling than at any other time, and always seemed more comfortable going somewhere overseas than returning home. Those were long hours aloft for him, like the nearly seven hours from Honolulu to Fiji, but he handled the extraordinary inconvenience and discomfort with admirable tolerance.

"Remember the first time I went to Viet Nam?" I asked him, as we jet-thrusted across the Pacific. "You were so nervous to let me go. But we saw in God's Word that Saigon was just as safe as Atlanta, as long as I went there in the will of God. It's the same now with you, Buddy, as you travel overseas."

"Yeah," he agreed.

The people of Sydney were absolutely wonderful to him, sparing no courtesy or consideration on his behalf.

"These people could help lift a lot of the financial load," I explained to him. "And they are really people of prayer."

Our national youth organization in Australia, an extremely vital group, named Johnny their permanent chairman and sent ideas to him for reaction and evaluation.

In the autumn of 1974, almost against her better judgment, Chris went with me on another journey "down under." Johnny had brightened considerably, and Mother Barker and Christina were so careful and capable with him that we felt we could leave him home with them.

Whether it was loneliness for us, or disappointment at not being able to make the trip, or simply the continuing onslaught of his terminal condition, I don't know. But Johnny had a rough time.

Then an urgent message came from Mother Barker. Because of an acute intestinal block, Johnny had been rushed to the hospital. His condition grew so severe that death could occur at any moment. I was heavily involved in responsibility and opportunity. Yet, as would any husband and father, I told Chris I would return to the States with her.

"You can't," she said. "It could be disastrous for you to leave your work here just now." She went home alone.

Within a few hours after her departure, I received word from an associate that Johnny's condition had worsened, so I followed her home by twenty-four hours. Johnny survived, but the load of concern grew heavier and heavier upon my heart.

In 1973, I had spoken at Moody Founder's Week, after which I was to leave for India. But Johnny became so ill we took him to the hospital. We had moments of apprehension about his life.

"I'm canceling the trip to India," I told Chris.

"You can't," she countered. "Johnny misses you terribly when you go. We all know that. But he and I have talked it over, and he doesn't ever want you to curtail your work on our account. If the Lord takes him home, we can always get you back in time for the funeral.

"What happens in the theater if an actor takes sick?" she continued. "Do they cancel the show? Well, our mandate is much more authoritative than theirs, our purpose ever so much higher. We have no recourse. You must go."

So I did. And, wonderfully, the Lord touched Johnny's body the very next day.

I wrote to Chris from Calcutta. I told her, "I've loved you for almost thirty years, but I want you to know I love you more right now and respect you more than ever before."

In 1974 Johnny again had to be hospitalized and his mother's time with me overseas was cut short. The impact of that crisis took an even deeper toll on my attitude. "We've talked and talked about moving to Hawaii," I said. "It would be far more central for my work. I need to travel to the Third World just as much as I need to be in the States. You and Johnny could live in Hawaii. It's like a paradise for him. So let's not talk about it anymore, let's do it."

So many times it has fallen to Chris's lot to be the spoiler, holding out for what she knew would be best, considering Johnny's condition. This time, although she felt deeply pessimistic about Johnny's future, she offered no contest.

I went to Johnny's bedside, took his hands, and said, "I've got great news for you, Buddy. The doctor tells us you've got several weeks of recuperating to do. But as soon as you're strong enough, I want us all to move to Hawaii."

Johnny's eyes widened in joy and anticipation.

"I mean it," I continued. "We'll move to Honolulu permanently."

The anticipation was good for Johnny, though Chris cautioned me that it was most unlikely he would ever be strong enough to tolerate travel again. He showed some improvement in December and on into January, and it was of much encouragement to him. But it was only temporary improvement. The last assault against his health had been definitive. He had bright days but overall grew increasingly listless. He was in constant, cruel pain.

"I shouldn't have gone on that last trip overseas," I said.

"Don't torment yourself," Chris told me.

"But you know how Johnny suffers whenever I go away."

"It's exactly the way he wanted it. He loves your ministry. He wants all of us to be as much a part of it as we can. If you should have stayed home last winter, then you should have stayed home again and again during the past twenty-four years. If you had followed that course, what could possibly have been accomplished in comparison to the ministry as it is now?"

I did a lot of thinking as we watched Johnny grow increasingly weaker. I remembered the earlier years —for instance, my concern over whether or not sin in my life had caused Johnny's situation. That was when the Holy Spirit led me to that event in John's Gospel where Jesus was asked about a man blind from his birth. Had he sinned? His parents?

"Neither," Jesus answered to both questions. The man's blindness was allowed by a wise heavenly Father so that the words of God might be made manifest in him.

I thought of verses like Hebrews 5:8, which says of Jesus, "Though he were a Son, yet learned he obedience by the things which he suffered."

I wondered if Johnny didn't touch more lives through his suffering than I have in all my years of ministry. I thought of men like Dr. Porter Barrington, so moved by Johnny's ministry he got nearly 900 people to send cards to him one Christmas. I thought of Johnny's loyalties. He was a hundred-percenter, that boy. He was all out for his pastor, all out for his friends, all out for his mother, for me, our ministry, friends like Christina, loved ones like Mother Barker, my father and mother.

Those first weeks into 1975 I kept as close to home and the office as possible, spending every available moment with my son. February ninth I needed to make a trip to Chattanooga.

"I see no reason why you shouldn't go," Chris told me. So I went. But that night I called home.

"Johnny's not well at all," she said.

"How sick is he?" I asked.

"Very."

I rushed back home.

"Johnny," I said, as I stepped to his bedside, "you got a cold, Buddy?"

Johnny could barely look up at me.

"As soon as you can snap out of it," I continued, "we're going to make that move to Honolulu."

Johnny's lips puckered faintly, the way he would do when something disappointed him. He knew it could never be. I stepped away.

"He's suffering terribly," Chris whispered to me, "and he's very weak."

Those next days dragged interminably. We maintained round-the-clock vigil. Instead of keeping in touch by phone from the office, I kept in touch with the office from our home.

Dr. Gibbs, our family physician, visited Johnny

daily. He did everything he could to alleviate Johnny's pain.

"He hardly sleeps at all," we told the doctor. "He's so uncomfortable and has so much pain."

It was pathetic to see our son so emaciated, unable to take any nourishment. He tossed his head back and forth, moaning, and when we spoke to him he would try his best to manage a smile.

"Do you want to take him to the hospital?" the doctor asked.

"Should we?"

"Well, frankly, about all the hospital could do would be to delay things some."

I looked at Johnny and turned away.

"Would it make it any easier on you, Mrs. Haggai?"

"No, Doctor," my wife replied. "I gave him up months ago. Just let him stay here. He's happier at home."

And that wise doctor agreed.

That thirteenth day of February dragged on. Then came the night. We all continued our vigil. It was Christina who remained most constant at his side. She scarcely left him even for a moment. She held his hand and stroked it, whispering, "It won't be too long now, Johnny, until everything will be all right."

As the night dragged on, Chris suggested that we try to be as quiet as possible in order not to upset Johnny in any way. We all slipped into an adjoining room, where we could monitor his movements or outcries but give him maximum silence.

I stayed away as long as I could, which was merely moments, and then returned to Johnny's side. I took both of his hands as I had so often done in our times of communication. They felt clammy to my grasp. "Johnny," I whispered, "I want to tell you something wonderful." I reached for my Bible. Then I read the twenty-first chapter of Revelation to him, keeping one of my hands on one of his.

> *And God shall wipe away all tears from their eyes;*
> *and there shall be no more death, neither sorrow,*
>   *nor crying,*
> *neither shall there be any more pain;*
> *for the former things are passed away.*

I know he heard because I saw a slight flicker of his eyes. I felt him try to squeeze my hand in affirming response.

Midnight came. Dr. Gibbs joined us again.

Johnny went downhill very quickly.

"I don't know how he can remain conscious," the doctor told me. "With all that pain, he should have been comatose before now."

The telltale rattle appeared in Johnny's throat.

I leaned over and whispered, "Can you hear me, Johnny?"

Johnny opened one eyelid just a little bit.

I took his hand again. "He's trying to pull my hand toward him," I said.

His breathing grew rapidly weaker, his face more jaundiced. Then, at two o'clock in the morning, the discomfort and ignominy which had marked his life —that terrible nemesis of vomiting—once more asserted itself as he emitted two pints of dark blood, took one last breath, and was gone.

"Thank God," Chris said with a composed voice, "he's free at last!"

Christina broke into tears. So did Mother Barker. But a deep and beautiful peace came over both Chris and me. "Now he knows how much we loved him," I whispered to my wife. "In heaven he knows. He knows."

We gathered around his bed. I offered a brief prayer of thanksgiving to God for the blessing Johnny had brought to our lives.

Christina clasped his hand once more, stroking it. Then we all turned and moved away into the other room.

We had Johnny dressed for burial in his favorite sweater, one Christina had given him. None of us lingered at the casket. We knew our boy was gone, only the shell remaining. But there was something very beautiful about that shell. The pain gone, the frustration, now completely relaxed in death, Johnny looked like a young executive, not like someone who had just finished nearly a quarter of a century of incessant suffering.

Dr. Bill Smith, our dear friend through the years, flew in from Honolulu to assist our pastor, Dr. Russell Dilday, in conducting the Saturday funeral. Then he returned home. Because of the weekend, burial was delayed until Monday. Somehow, through a mix-up in communications, our pastor, who was to have conducted the brief interment service at the cemetery, failed to appear.

It may well have been by God's own design for my personal enrichment.

We waited a few brief moments. I doubt if our friends, who had gathered there with us, realized our concern. Because, as though it had been scheduled, I stepped up to the graveside.

"It is our solemn and unhappy responsibility to commit this body to the ground," I said slowly, "as it has been our solemn and happy responsibility to have already committed his soul to heaven through the merits of the shed blood of Jesus Christ. Jesus said, "I am the resurrection and the life; he that believeth in me, though he were dead, yet shall he live; and whosoever liveth and believeth in me shall never die.""

Then I offered a brief prayer, carefully measuring each word, my soul torn with sorrow.

As soon as it could be arranged we had a simple marker placed at the grave. It reads:

JOHN EDMUND HAGGAI, JR.

AFTERWORD

SUCH a lonely place our house became, especially for Chris. Little by little she put Johnny's things away. We disposed of the hospital bed, took down the rigging in the bathroom, altered the large room in which Chris had cared for Johnny for so many years. Christina stayed on a few days and then returned to Belfast. "I'm what I have become," she said, gripping my wife's hand and weeping, "because of you and Johnny. When I first came, when I would feel so sorry for myself, I would look at Johnny. How he suffered so patiently. How he never complained. How he smiled so beautifully. And I would be ashamed. And then you would help me to accept myself, to see myself as God's special creation. Thank you."

How will this change my life, my ministry, I wondered. Who is going to pick up the immense prayer support Johnny gave? How many victories did we win because of his prayers? And what problems and challenges must we face in the future without his prayers? As you know, I am convinced that no one, no matter how interested in our ministry to the Third World, upheld me so consistently and so effectively as did Johnny right from the initial phases.

For us, heaven has become a brighter, a more longed-for place, though we aren't morbid about it.

God is wonderfully opening doors of opportunity and service for Chris. She knows Johnny would have wanted her to enter those doors and to serve with all her might.

I like to think of our son in heaven, walking and running at last. What an enormous victory it must be for someone like him, to have been a lifelong prisoner in a body wracked with discomfort and pain and then to find release in the horizonless vistas of eternity.

I miss him.

Terribly, sometimes.

But Johnny is free, free at last, and like his mother, I thank God.

HAGGAI INSTITUTE

Billions of people live in nations where evangelism by outsiders is discouraged or openly prohibited. Haggai Institute selects Christians of proven influence from within these nations; equips them to reach their own people for Christ; and enables them to reproduce their training in others.

To achieve this, Haggai Institute utilizes two strategically located centers in Singapore and Maui and a top-grade faculty drawn almost exclusively from the non-Western world. Its program provides in-depth, small-group lectures and workshops on the "how" of evangelism. It also provides unique consultative resources through which participating leaders draw up their own individual strategies for evangelism.

Since 1969, more than 30,000 Christian leaders have graduated from Haggai Institute's international, regional, and national seminars. These men and women represent almost all denominations and vocations across Asia, Africa, and Latin America and are serving in more than 150 nations. Each is engaged in active personal evangelism, and on average will pass the training on to 100 other leaders.

For more information on the Haggai Institute ministry of world evangelism, write to: P.O.Box 13; Atlanta, Georgia 30370, U.S.A.

ABOUT THE AUTHOR

John Edmund Haggai has spent a lifetime studying and teaching leadership.

As Founder, Chairman, and CEO of Haggai Institute, he travels extensively every year and has circled the globe 82 times. He counts among his friends many of the world's most distinguished and illustrious leaders.

He is a prolific writer. His first book, *How to Win Over Worry*, has been a bestseller since 1959 and is now published in over 15 languages. Among his other books are:*How to Win Over Pain, The Leading Edge, Lead On!, Paul J. Meyer and the Art of Giving, and Be Careful What You Call Impossible.*

With a reputation as an informative and captivating speaker, Dr. Haggai is sought after by international investment bankers on Wall Street and by graduate students at Yale. His audiences have included the world's largest Rotary Club; the Kiwanis International Convention; the Institute for Human Development in Seoul, Korea; and numerous civic clubs and universities across six continents.

Dr. Haggai was born in Louisville, Kentucky, and lives in Atlanta, Georgia. But his heart is in the Third World, and his vision embraces leadership and evangelism in every nation on earth.